MARGARET HAMILTON

FROM CLEVELAND, OHIO

TO THE LAND OF OZ

DON BILLIE

Copyright © 2024 by Don Billie

All rights reserved.

No portion of this book may be reproduced in any form without written permission from the publisher or author except as permitted by U.S. copyright law.

This publication is designed to provide accurate and authoritative information in regard to the subject matter covered. It is sold with the understanding that neither the author nor the publisher is engaged in rendering legal, investment, accounting, or other professional services. While the publisher and author have used their best efforts in preparing this book, they make no representations or warranties with respect to the accuracy or completeness of the contents of this book and specifically disclaim any implied warranties of merchantability or fitness for a particular purpose. No warranty may be created or extended by sales representatives or written sales materials. The advice and strategies contained herein may not be suitable for your situation. You should consult with a professional when appropriate. Neither the publisher nor the author shall be liable for any loss of profit or any other commercial damages, including but not limited to special, incidental, consequential, personal, or other damages.

Illustrations by Julia Ruprecht

First edition 2024

TABLE OF CONTENTS

PROLOGUE 1

INTRODUCTION 7

1 THERE'S NO PLACE LIKE HOME 13

2 WE'RE OFF TO WHEELOCK COLLEGE! 40

3 CLEVELAND PLAY HOUSE APPRENTICE 58

4 LIONS AND TIGERS AND BROADWAY (OH MY!) 90

5 I HAVE A FEELING WE'RE NOT IN
   KANSAS ANYMORE! 111

6 MAKING A WICKED WITCH 127

7 WITCHY WOMAN 148

8 MISS GULCH 169

9 ITS FUNNY, BUT I FEEL AS IF I'VE KNOWN YOU
   ALL THE TIME 175

10 AFTER OZ 195

11 NEW YORK NEW YORK 227

12 BROADWAY AND A SONG (OR TWO) 250

13 THE KINDEST OF WITCHES 266

14 THERE'S NO PLACE LIKE HOME - PART 2 291

15 FINAL TRIP DOWN THE YELLOW BRICK ROAD 310

16 BEWITCHING LEGACY 331

17 MYTHS, RUMORS, AND MISCELLANEOUS 350

ACKNOWLEDGEMENTS 359

SOURCES 363

PROLOGUE

Little did I realize years ago, when I was in college writing for the aptly named *Cleveland State Cauldron*, that I'd one day be authoring a biography about the Wicked Witch of the West – Cleveland's Margaret Hamilton. And that the effort to do so would take over two decades!

On a Niagara Falls family vacation years ago, we visited the usual tourist places, including a kitschy wax museum. I wondered why Cleveland had nothing like that back home. Both Cleveland and, more so, Ohio had lots of entertaining and historical people to fill a wax museum.

Only Ohio, as the "Birthplace of Aviation" (the Wright brothers), along with ground-breaking astronauts John Glenn and Neil Armstrong, could boast of being home to such historical figures, along with the likes of Jesse Owens. Add in Ohio entertainers such as Clark Gable, Dean Martin, Halle Berry, and Drew Carey, to name just a few, plus such scoundrels as Charles Manson and Jeffrey Dahmer, and Superman's creators Jerry Siegel and Joe Shuster, and you had quite an ensemble! **And the Wicked Witch of the West herself – Cleveland's Margaret Hamilton!**

Acting on a whim, I developed the idea of creating a fun yet educational, non-profit Ohio-themed wax museum in Cleveland back in 2001 and ran with it. The Ohio Wax Museum concept was born after forming a non-profit, along with a requisite Board of Directors composed of local business folks/friends (thanks again to John and Carol, among others).

Over the next few years (2002 – 2005), museum development focused on obtaining funding from Cleveland's politicians and local foundations, along with publicizing the effort in Cleveland's newspapers and magazines. A great article supporting the museum appeared in *The Plain Dealer* by legendary gonzo writer Michael Heaton (aka The Minister of Culture), even featured a photo of me "riding" on the back of the broom with Margaret Hamilton/Wicked Witch of the West.

Actress Margaret Hamilton, who played the Wicked Witch of the West in *The Wizard of Oz*, got her start at the Cleveland Play House. Don Billie says she'd be an obvious choice for an Ohio wax museum.

Myself (a much younger version) and Margaret Hamilton circa 2002

As part of their development, The Ohio Wax Museum collected information about the people to be showcased. I chatted with the head of DC Comics, the daughter of Jesse Owens, the amazing people at NASA, and Charles Manson's biographer (who offered to connect me with Charlie). Carol from our board got a chance to meet the legend of the Cleveland Browns, Jim Brown.

I spoke with Hamilton (Ham) Meserve, Margaret Hamilton's son, who is both a successful businessperson and a friendly individual. I also met and spoke with people from several organizations connected to Margaret:

Cleveland Play House, the Junior League of Cleveland, and Hathaway Brown, where she went to school.

In 2005, The Ohio Wax Museum hosted a well-attended exhibit at Cleveland's Tower City complex featuring a Wicked Witch figure with accompanying detailed information about Margaret Hamilton. Despite the exhibit doing well, the museum didn't get the funding needed to advance it further and had to stop the development process.

Shortly after stopping The Ohio Wax Museum development effort in 2005, I realized I had accumulated an amazing amount of information about Margaret Hamilton – more than enough to put together a biography. I couldn't believe it when I found out that there had never been a biography written about Margaret.

Over the next two years, I conducted additional research about Margaret and worked on a draft biography about her. In 2007, I contacted Margaret's son (Ham Meserve) again to inform him of my biography effort, as well as ask for additional information on a few topics about her. Much to my surprise, Ham informed me that his son Scott Meserve (Margaret's grandson) was also working on a

Margaret Hamilton biography that would be published soon.

I was caught off guard by Ham's feedback. I expected that he'd be pleased someone was finally doing a biography about his mom, but there was not much more discussion at that point. The feedback from the questions I had hoped to discuss with Ham about Margaret went unanswered.[1]

It made little sense for me to publish a Margaret Hamilton biography at the same time her grandson would do so, and I put my book effort on hold in 2007.

Fast forward to 2024, and for whatever reason, Margaret's grandson, Scott Meserve, never published a biography about her. So, I have dusted off my 2007 draft, made a few updates, and created the *first-ever* book about **Margaret Hamilton**. I hope you enjoy it.

---

[1] In a March 12, 2009, *Beverly Hills Weekly* interview, Ham Meserve restated what he told me on the telephone earlier: "Scott is currently collecting material to write her biography."

DISCLAIMER: I do not consider myself an Oz expert – there are many excellent authors (such as Michael Patrick Hearn, John Fricke, Bill Stillman, Jay Scarfone, and Aljean Harmetz to name a few) who have written some amazing books about *The Wizard of Oz*, and social media Oz historians such as Ryan Jay, Tori Calamito, and Andrew Bonomolo who know far more on the topic than I ever will.

INTRODUCTION

Margaret Hamilton's role as the Wicked Witch of the West landed her in fourth place on the American Film Institute's "100 Greatest Heroes and Villains" list, right behind Hannibal Lecter, Anthony Perkins' *Psycho*, and Darth Vader.

Who was Margaret Hamilton? To those closest to her, she was simply "Maggie."

How did a young Cleveland kindergarten teacher come to portray the scariest character ever known to young children?

How ironic is it she coincidentally had a sister named "Dorothy?"

One of the greatest character actresses of all time, Margaret Hamilton, appeared in countless movies, radio, television, and stage performances throughout her lengthy career. Appearing in *The Wizard of Oz* for a mere 12 minutes as the terrifying Wicked Witch, Margaret established herself as one of the top movie villains of all time.

Margaret Hamilton's life was a wonderful celebration of a woman whose kind personality starkly contrasted her evil Wicked Witch of the West persona. The most enduring paradox of Margaret's life was the fact that she truly loved children and was both a kindergarten and nursery school teacher before her Wicked Witch depiction. She was also a single mother raising a young son following an all too brief marriage while trying to maintain an acting career.

Margaret's kindness to her fans was legendary, as she diligently would respond to fan mail, often including a signed photo. If someone was lucky enough to have crossed paths with Margaret, she always took time to talk with them – especially youngsters.

Stories about the filming of *The Wizard of Oz* have detailed how a lonely young Judy Garland's only adult friend during the filming was Margaret – a friendship they maintained over the years.

Margaret never forgot her roots and remained an avid supporter of her hometown of Cleveland, Ohio.

Over the years, there have been countless books written about *The Wizard of Oz*, as well as many biographies of Oz celebrities - there's even a biography dedicated to Toto! We've been waiting far too long for a book that captures Margaret Hamilton's trip to the Land of Oz.

> *"I've frightened more children than practically anyone else. It always seems too funny to me because I love children so much."*
>
> **- Margaret Hamilton**

Margaret Hamilton

Dedicated to my wife and family

- and -

in memory of

Margaret Hamilton

1
THERE'S NO PLACE LIKE HOME

In a cozy Cleveland classroom, young Cleveland kindergarten teacher Margaret Hamilton animatedly read the final passage of *The Wonderful Wizard of Oz* to her enthralled students: "Aunt Em had just come out of the house to water the cabbages when she looked up and saw Dorothy running toward her. 'My darling child!' she cried, folding the little girl in her arms, and covering her face with kisses; 'where in the world did you come from?' 'From the Land of Oz,' said Dorothy gravely. 'And here is Toto, too. And Aunt Em! I'm so glad to be at home again.'"

Her students, eyes wide with wonder, leaned forward, captivated by the story. Much like her students, Margaret had also enjoyed listening to the classic L. Frank Baum's novel as a young child. In Margaret's case, she fondly recalled her mother reading the classic tale. As she finished reading to her class, little did Margaret know her own destiny was closely tied to this magical tale.

✦ ✤ ✦

On the chilly day of December 9, 1902, Margaret Brainard Hamilton was born in Cleveland, Ohio. It was a time when the city was bustling with growth and opportunity, fueled by booming industries and a surge in population. As Cleveland flourished, so did the Hamilton family's prominence in the community.

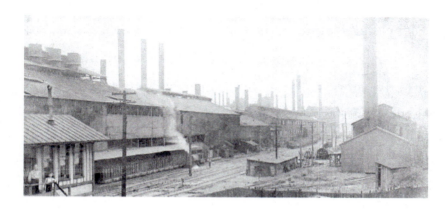

Cleveland's industry expands rapidly at the turn of the century

Growing up in Cleveland, newly christened as 'The Sixth City' following the 1910 census, Margaret witnessed firsthand the city's dynamic transformation. She fondly recalled the bustling streets, filled with the sounds of progress and the promise of opportunity.

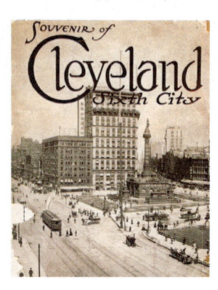

Cleveland's rapid industrial growth sparked a cultural renaissance, transforming the city into a vibrant hub for the arts. Theaters, galleries, and music halls sprang up, catering to the city's burgeoning population. Among these new institutions were The Cleveland Play House and the Hanna Theatre, where Margaret would eventually leave her mark.

Cleveland Play House's 86th Street Theatre opened in 1927

Hanna Theatre after 1921 opening
(marquee on left slightly obscured by utility pole)

One of the plays in the Hanna Theatre's inaugural 1921 season was *Toto*. It's interesting to note that this name is forever associated with Margaret Hamilton, who played Miss Gulch and the Wicked Witch of the West in *The Wizard of Oz*. This connection is quite a coincidence, considering that Margaret would one day appear at the theater.

Toto, the 1921 Hanna Theatre play, and Toto with Dorothy in Oz

Even before Cleveland's rapid growth, the Hamilton family enjoyed a distinguished place within the city. Margaret's grandfather, the Honorable Edwin Hamilton, was a well-known judge who served on the bench for many years in Cleveland. Presiding as a judge for the Cuyahoga County Court of Common Pleas, Edwin had a reputation as a fair and decisive magistrate.

Judge Edwin Hamilton – Margaret's grandfather

Walter Jones (W. J.) Hamilton, Margaret's father, was a distinguished attorney in Cleveland. Known for his meticulous approach and keen legal mind, he carried on the family tradition with pride, practicing law in the bustling heart of the city.

After earning his law degree from Cornell in 1890, he was admitted to the Ohio Bar later that year. In 1891, he collaborated with W. C. Ong to form the successful Cleveland law firm Ong & Hamilton. W. J. was best known as a legal counselor and rarely took part in trial or court work. He gained a reputation for being of a retiring nature and for not joining social clubs. A lawyer friend commented about W. J., "He realized the law was a jealous mistress and for that reason devoted his time to it."

After Margaret's grandfather, the Honorable Edwin Hamilton, retired as a judge, he collaborated with his son W. J. to form the law firm of Hamilton, Hamilton, and Smith in downtown Cleveland's New England Building, better known later as the National City Bank Building.

RETIRED JUDGE / ATTORNEY EDWIN T. HAMILTON

ATTORNEY WALTER J. HAMILTON

HAMILTON, HAMILTON, & SMITH

NEW ENGLAND BUILDING
AKA
NATIONAL CITY BANK BUILDING

THE law firm of Hamilton, Hamilton & Smith, formed May 1st, 1896, consisting of E. T. Hamilton, W. J. Hamilton and H. D. Smith, have opened offices for the general practice of law, at their rooms, Nos. 409 and 410, New England Bldg., Euclid av., this city.

Margaret's mother, the former Jennie M. Adams of Cleveland, was a musician from her earliest days. She played the piano in public recitals as a young girl and later worked as a music teacher until she and W. J. were married in 1891.

Just how prominent the Hamilton family was in Cleveland is clear by the extensive coverage their marriage received in the city's newspaper, *The Plain Dealer*. The end of the article notes how Judge Hamilton (and his wife) gave Margaret's parents a house at 68 Tilden Avenue for their wedding present.

HAPPILY MARRIED.

The Marguerite Wedding of Miss Jennie Adams and Mr. Walter Hamilton— Evening Reception.

The marriage of Miss Jennie M. Adams, daughter of Mrs. M. J. Adams, to Mr. Walter J. Hamilton, was solemnized at 7:30 o'clock last evening at the Euclid Avenue Baptist church. The church has recently been refitted so that much decoration would be out of place. The rostrum was banked with tall tree palms and clumps of marguerites, which flowers were used almost exclusively in the decorations and bouquets and gave name to the wedding.

The guests entered to music by Miss Marguerete Wuertz and Mr. James H. Rogers, organist. At the approach of the bridal party the organ notes alone were heard shading into the Lohengrin march. The ushers, Mr. Holmes Marshall, Mr. Frank Quayle, Mr. Edgar Mitchell and Mr. Charles Clark, preceded the bridal party down the aisle to the altar. Four little flower girls, Misses Florence Adams, a cousin of the bride; Edith Smith, Gertrude Hatch and May Quinby, followed. They wore Watteau dresses of white silk mulle, garlanded with marguerites and carried huge branches of the flower.

After them came Miss Louise Leslie and Miss Maude Thayer, the bridesmaids, attired in Watteau gowns of white silk and carrying bouquets of daisies and white carnations. The maid of honor was Miss Mable Adams, a cousin of the bride. She wore a Watteau gown of white bengaline with pearl girdle.

Miss Adams entered next with her brother, Mr. Charles E. Adams, who gave her away. She wore a Watteau gown of heavy white satin with pearl and crystal trimmings. Her bouquet was of bride roses and maidenhair fern. She was met at the altar by Mr. Hamilton, who was attended by Mr. Mulford Wade. Rev. J. C. Applegarth, pastor of the church, performed the ceremony.

Repairing to the home of Mrs. Adams at No. 34 Granger street, supper was served to the bridal party. From 8:30 o'clock to 11 a reception was given by Mr. and Mrs. Hamilton to nearly 200 of their friends. The house was tastefully decorated with large bunches of marguerites, white carnations and garlands of smilax.

A little before midnight Mr. and Mrs. Hamilton left on a short southern tour. Upon their return they will begin housekeeping at No. 68 Tilden avenue in their new home given them as a wedding gift by Judge Edwin T. and Mrs. Hamilton.

The Hamilton family home on Tilden Avenue was situated a few miles east of the winding Cuyahoga River, not too far from Cleveland's flourishing cultural environs downtown, and less than a mile from nearby University Circle.

Following their marriage, Margaret's mother, Jennie, set aside her music career to raise their three girls (Gladys, Dorothy, and Margaret) and one boy (Edwin). Margaret was the youngest child and was born while her family was still living at 68 Tilden Avenue in the home given to her parents as a wedding gift.

Cleveland rebranded Tilden Avenue as East 84th Street in 1906 as part of their effort to assign numerical street names to most north-south roads, resulting in the street no longer existing.

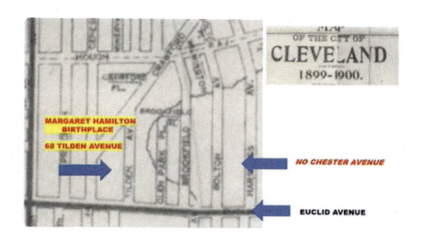

Margaret Hamilton's first residence at 68 Tilden Avenue pre-1906

The later creation of a new major thoroughfare, Chester Avenue, resulted in the demolition of the home.

[23]

Few people in Cleveland realize they're literally driving by the location where Margaret Hamilton once lived as they commute down busy Chester Avenue.

Margaret Hamilton's birthplace today in Cleveland is at the intersection of Chester Avenue and East 84th Street

The Hamilton family moved to 2058 East 96th Street, just south of Euclid Avenue, when Margaret was a young child. At the time, nearby Euclid Avenue was still known as "Millionaires' Row," populated with lavish mansions and touted as "the most beautiful street in the world," often drawing comparisons to the Champs-Élysées in Paris.

Drury Mansion on "Millionaire's Row"
near the Hamilton home still exists today

Sadly, once again, there is no trace of the home on East 96th where Margaret grew up.

Margaret Hamilton's childhood home, 2058 East 96th Street

When the world-renowned Cleveland Clinic began its massive growth, the clinic razed Margaret's home, along with several blocks in the neighborhood.

The world-renowned Cleveland Clinic now occupies
the location where the Hamilton family home once stood

The Hamiltons were not only a prominent family in Cleveland, but very active in the city's social scene. People described Margaret's mother, Jennie, as giving an impression of great vitality. She displayed a lively and enthusiastic demeanor. Jennie had a peculiarly sympathetic understanding of little children, a trait that Margaret would share as she grew up.

Once the children grew up years later, Jennie resumed an active social and civic life in Cleveland. Renewing her interest in music, she was a member of the Lecture-Recital Club and the Fortnightly Musical Club. She served as president of the women's board of St. Luke's Hospital and was president of the women's guild of Calvary Presbyterian Church.

Jennie's social events were often noted
in the local newspaper's "Social News of the Week"

As parents, W. J. and Jennie tried to instill a sense of community service as part of the Hamilton children's upbringing. The girls' later involvement in various local causes (primarily through The Junior League of Cleveland) was a direct reflection of their parents' desire for them to help their less fortunate fellow citizens.

Margaret's community service efforts led her to be active with many causes throughout her lifetime - she was never too busy to lend her time to what she felt was a good cause.

Margaret shared her service-oriented upbringing with reporter Holly Hill, "My grandmother, who was very active in the temperance movement and in the Baptist church, got my two sisters and brother and me started in community activities."

"At age 12, I started working in a babies dispensary at a hospital. I was always crazy about children. I learned how to feed premature babies with a medicine dropper, and I just loved that. I worked Saturdays, and I must have been a reliable child because they often called me to come in after school."

"A little later on, my oldest sister Dorothy taught classes at a settlement house in a poor Italian community (Cleveland's 'Big Italy'), and I helped her. Then I taught my own cooking and dramatic classes there while I was in high school."

Margaret and her sister volunteered in Cleveland's "Big Italy" neighborhood

Margaret's older brother Edwin zoomed across the sky as a pilot in World War I long before his sister would do so as the Wicked Witch of the West. Edwin joined the British Royal Flying Corps with a strong desire to serve the cause of freedom, as the United States didn't join the war until near the end. Following that, Edwin pursued a career as a magazine editor and authored many children's aviation and aircraft crafts books.

Captain Edwin T. Hamilton

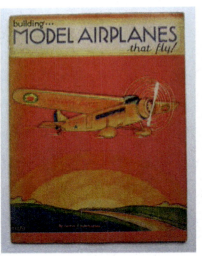

Edwin T. Hamilton books

Margaret's oldest sister, Dorothy, had the highest public profile of her siblings. Dorothy married Charles Brush Jr., the heir to Charles Brush, who was a millionaire industrialist, renowned philanthropist, and one of the inventors of commercial lighting. Charles Brush Jr. passed away in his early 30s, leaving Dorothy Hamilton Brush in charge of a large inheritance. She became the primary administrator of the Brush Foundation in Cleveland.

Dorothy helped to found The Maternal Health Association in Cleveland, the city's first birth control clinic and the predecessor to Planned Parenthood of Cleveland. Dorothy was close friends with Margaret Sanger, the early president of International Planned Parenthood, who devoted her life to legalizing birth control and making it universally available for women.

Margaret Sanger and Dorothy Hamilton Brush

As a philanthropist, Dorothy donated some property near Cleveland for what is now Furnace Run Park in Richfield in the Summit Metro Parks in honor of her husband, Charles Brush Jr.

Dorothy Hamilton Brush at Furnace Run Park Brushwood boulder dedication

Of her siblings, Margaret was closest to sister Gladys, who would one day be matron of honor at her wedding. Gladys moved to Columbus and was later president of the Columbus Junior League. Like her sister Margaret, Gladys dabbled in the theater and even appeared on Broadway in 1928 with the Players Club of Columbus in *Trifles* as Mrs. Peters at the Frolic Theatre.

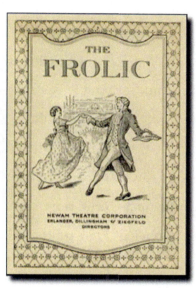

Gladys Hamilton Mohler once performed at Broadway's Frolic Theatre

As for Margaret, by all accounts, she had a happy childhood. During visits home over the years coinciding with her appearances at The Cleveland Play House, she often recalled a few of the simple joys of her childhood, sharing fond memories with local newspaper writers:

"There was a crab apple tree in our yard, and I remember making great piles of crab apples and my mother making jelly out of them this time of the year (October). You don't come across crab apple jelly so much anymore. And one year, we had an excess, and we loaded a little red wagon with the crab apples and took them out to sell."

"I did the usual things little girls did in those days. I took singing and dancing lessons, but I was happy enough just growing up. I lived on Tilden Avenue. I think it became East 84th Street; then, our family moved to East 96th Street. I grew up around here, at 96th and Cedar, where the Cleveland Clinic now stands, and I remember going to the movies at East 105th and Euclid when it only cost a nickel."

The Cleveland schools Margaret attended as a young girl a century ago still exist today, though both have moved from their original settings.

"I went to Bolton School, and I can remember when I was six or seven how they would repair the cobblestones on the street. There were these pools of tar, and you would stick your finger in it to get some and chew on it. I recall that it tasted quite good."

Margaret attended Bolton Elementary School, then at East 90th and Carnegie Avenue

Margaret was so fond of her kindergarten and first-grade teachers at Bolton School, she wanted to follow their example. Commenting on her early desire to be a schoolteacher, she said, "I was born loving devotedly – first my dolls, then babies and children (little ones)."

Bolton Elementary School also had another famous student a few years after Margaret – Jesse Owens, who would make Olympic history in track and field and was known as "The Buckeye Bullet."

Jesse Owens (with fellow sprinter Ralph Metcalfe) also attended Bolton Elementary School

Margaret later attended Hathaway Brown School, a prestigious private all-girls prep school, then located near her home on East 97th Street. Founded in 1876, Hathaway Brown is the oldest surviving private girls' school in the Cleveland area. Early on, she helped in the kindergarten at Hathaway Brown and later enjoyed being a cheerleader for the girls' basketball team.

Hathaway Brown's motto, "Where Girls Soar," was prophetic when Margaret later soared across the sky as the Wicked Witch of the West

Hathaway Brown School (original location by East 97th Street)

Hathaway Brown School 1921 yearbook
graduation photograph of Margaret Hamilton

Margaret's yearbook noted she was nicknamed "Ham," favorite word was "golly," and was class Vice President.

A milestone in young Margaret's life occurred when she portrayed an elder Englishman, Sir Peter Antrobus, in Hathaway Brown's senior play *Pomander Walk*.

Margaret Hamilton (by lamppost with eye patch) as Sir Peter Antrobus in the Hathaway Brown 1921 senior play *Pomander Walk*

Leading up to the play, Margaret took singing and acting lessons for several years from Cleveland voice teacher Grace Probert, who recognized her talent and "kept after me to make singing and acting my vocation. She kept hounding me until I decided maybe I should go to New York and attend an acting school. The problem was announcing my decision to my family."

Encouraged by her voice teacher and the applause of friends and family from her role in *Pomander Walk*, Margaret told her parents that she would like to pursue acting instead of going to college to become a kindergarten teacher.

"You'll do no such thing," her mother replied. "You'll go to Wheelock (a kindergarten training school), as you've always wanted to, and when you know how to earn your living, you can fool around with the theatre all you want to."

Though Margaret reluctantly relented and followed her mother's advice, the acting bug seed had been planted, and her long journey to the land of Oz had begun.

2
WE'RE OFF TO WHEELOCK COLLEGE!

Deferring to her parent's practical advice to pursue a career as a kindergarten teacher, Margaret went to Boston in the fall of 1921 to attend the prestigious Wheelock Kindergarten Training School.

Founded in 1888 (since renamed to Wheelock College), the Wheelock Kindergarten Training School offered classes created by Lucy Wheelock and was at the forefront of the kindergarten movement. Wheelock's innovative educational programs nurtured the bonds between children and families and stressed early childhood education as the solution to many societal problems.

Lucy Wheelock personally ensured that Margaret and her other students learned about the lives of poor immigrant families in Boston as part of Wheelock Kindergarten Training School's involvement with multicultural education.

Wheelock Kindergarten Training School in Boston

Margaret attended Wheelock Kindergarten Training School for two years, graduating in June 1923. Margaret took on leadership roles during her senior year, being elected as the class president and leading the Glee Club.

In return trips to Wheelock over the years, Margaret spoke proudly of her time there.

"I received such a fine foundation at Wheelock… really everything I needed to live by. Miss Wheelock was such a warm, friendly person – a marvelous combination of sweetness and gentleness with tremendous strength, determination, and high standards. No one could have been more charming. She appeared as fragile as a flower but possessed tremendous inner strength. We were all in awe of her, yet there was a feeling of deep affection."

"I remember most particularly two things she said: 'Best is the well-kept memory of a lovely thing' and 'When you have children, remember – your children do not *belong* to you – they are a loan from God to be loved, nurtured, guided, clothed, and then to let go.'"

Margaret credited her training at Wheelock with increasing her interest in children, which brightened and broadened her life. She felt that acting and teaching young children were the two "gifts" that she tried to develop over her lifetime.

Wheelock Kindergarten Training School 1923 yearbook photo

Wheelock did not distract Margaret from her passion for acting. Through her activities with the Glee Club, including organizing the Christmas concert and participation in Wheelock's senior play as Jo in *Little Women*, her zest for acting remained a constant even while in college.

Margaret (bottom left) in Wheelock's performance of *Little Women*

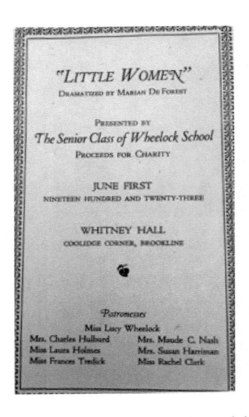

Margaret returned years later in 1978 to deliver Wheelock's commencement address – a mere 55 years after her graduation from the school. She spoke of her personal journey in her commencement speech: "For myself, when I am explaining my voyage from kindergarten teacher to actor, I always say, 'Inside every born teacher is a born actor, and inside every born actor is a born teacher.'"

Shortly after Margaret delivered Wheelock's commencement speech, she did another graduation speech at nearby Dana Hall High School in Wellesley, Massachusetts.

Margaret giving Dana Hall School commencement speech in 1978

After graduating from Wheelock in June 1923, Margaret went on vacation with her parents to Canada before starting work as a kindergarten teacher. Ever since she was a child, Margaret and her family took an annual summer vacation in Canada to escape Cleveland's summer heat, staying at the King Edward Hotel in Toronto before visiting other nearby destinations.

The Hamilton's 1923 Canadian vacation included a stay at the Wawa Hotel in Huntsville, Ontario, and became one of several fiery incidents in Margaret's lifetime. A deadly fire at the hotel broke out, with Margaret and her family narrowly escaping while several other hotel guests perished in the blaze.

Back home in Cleveland after her harrowing escape from the Canadian resort fire, Margaret began teaching kindergarten at Hough Elementary School for the 1923 – 1924 school year.

Hough Elementary School was on East 85th and Hough Avenue in Cleveland

[47]

Much like the two Cleveland homes Margaret grew up in that no longer exist, the same is true for Hough Elementary School. Years after she taught there, the school was a victim of arson.

Hough School Burns; Blamed on Vandalism

A fire believed started by vandals last night destroyed about half of Hough Elementary School, 1915 Hough Avenue N. E.

The blaze burned out an 81-year-old section of the 2½-story brick structure, one of the oldest public schools in the city.

Police said there were a few incidents in which young bystanders threw rocks and bottles at arriving firemen. But they were quickly dispersed and there was no serious troubles.

THERE WERE NO reports of injuries.
Damage was estimated at $110,000—including $10,000 damage to contents—by Assistant Fire Chief Matthew A. Fitzgerald. The arson squad will begin an investigation of the blaze today.

Paul W. Briggs, superintendent of Cleveland public schools, said it would cost about $45,000 per room to replace the 12 classrooms destroyed. This would place the cost of restoring the burned-out section at more than half-million dollars.

It was not known if that section would be replaced, but Briggs said a second section of the building which was damaged by smoke and heat would be restored this week. There will be no school for Hough School pupils today.

SCHOOL BURNS — An 81-year-old section of Hough Elementary School blazes as fireman atop snorkel truck trains hose on the flames. About half of the school was destroyed.

Following a brief teaching stint at Hough Elementary, Margaret channeled her passion for early childhood education into opening her own nursery school at the Cleveland Heights Presbyterian Church. The small classroom quickly filled with the sounds of children's laughter and learning, a testament to Margaret's dedication and enthusiasm. "I charged $100 a year," she noted in an interview. "My sister and my friends all sent their children. It was very successful."

Still, Margaret yearned for the stage, and she sought a teaching job that would allow her to be closer to the thriving theater scene of Broadway. Her job search resulted in Margaret getting a job as a kindergarten teacher for the 1926 – 1927 school year at Rye Country Day School in Rye, New York. Though she felt somewhat reluctant to leave her family in Cleveland, Margaret was excited at the opportunity to be close to the New York City theater scene.

On July 1, 1926, shortly after Margaret had accepted the teaching position at Rye Country Day School, her mother, Jennie, passed away. With a sad heart, she reluctantly went to her new kindergarten position in New York, some 30 miles from the lights of Broadway.

Reflecting on her time at Rye, Margaret remarked, "All the teachers lived together in a large residence. It reminded me of Shakespeare's line, 'get thee to a nunnery.' There wasn't a man in sight. We went to New York regularly and saw all the plays."

Wicked Witch
Margaret Hamilton, who played the Wicked Witch of the West in the film classic "The Wizard of Oz," delights Rye Country Day School students Thursday although missing her famous ruby slippers and the Yellow Brook Road.

After one year of teaching at Rye, Margaret returned home to Cleveland to help her widowed father. Returning to Cleveland, Margaret took on a position at a recently established nursery school in Bratenahl on Lakeshore Boulevard, which was founded by Caroline Brewer Goff, a fellow alumna of Hathaway Brown.

NOT kindergarten students of Margaret Hamilton!!

Many stories, both in print and online, claim that Margaret Hamilton was the kindergarten teacher of Jim Backus (of *Mr. Magoo* and *Gilligan's Island* fame) and Emmy Award-winning actor William Windom. This false narrative has sadly been spread across multiple platforms like Wikipedia, IMDb, YouTube, and various social media sites (Instagram, Facebook, Twitter, and TikTok).

The originator of the Jim Backus tale is unknown. Backus was born in 1913 and is indeed from Cleveland and attended kindergarten there. He would've been in kindergarten around 1918 when Margaret Hamilton was still in high school (she graduated from Hathaway Brown in 1921). Margaret then got her kindergarten credential from Wheelock College in 1923, meaning Backus would have had to be a 10-year-old kindergarten student the first year she taught kindergarten at Hough Elementary – meaning he obviously was not in her kindergarten class.

Jim Backus, aka Mr. Magoo and Mr. Howell,
was NOT a kindergarten student of Margaret Hamilton

The oft-repeated "feel good" William Windom kindergarten story (he retold it multiple times himself, including an interview on TCM) describes how they "discovered" their long-ago kindergarten connection while filming the movie *Brewster McCloud* together in 1970.

Windom recounted how they were "sitting there having dinner, and she's talking, talking – because she never shut up; she talked a mile a minute, and she mentions something about teaching at Rye Country Day, and I said, 'Hold it, Maggie! What do you mean Rye Country Day?'"

They figured it out. "Maggie!" Windom was bursting. "I couldn't believe it!" he said. "I jumped up and ran all over the dining room. Finally, when I settled down and sat, she stared at me with those beady little eyes, and she said, 'I think... I remember you.'"

If we look closer, Margaret taught at Rye Country Day School during the 1926 - 1927 school year and then returned home to help care for her widowed father in 1927. She was in The Cleveland Play House Apprenticeship Program from the fall of 1927 – 1930, with her name appearing in many playbills during those years. Windom, born in 1923, would have likely started kindergarten in 1928 at Rye (which he did attend). However, Windom would have been only two years old when the fall 1926 school year began in which Margaret taught at Rye before returning home – too young for him to be a kindergarten student.

Reviewing William Windom's memoir *Journeyman Actor* provides a slightly different version of him discovering he was a student of Margaret. "She told me that she had taught kindergarten before she became an actress. 'Where?' I asked. 'Rye Country Day School.' 'When?' 'Oh, 1928, 29, 30.' It turned out Margaret Hamilton had been my kindergarten teacher."

As noted above, Margaret was in the well-documented Cleveland Play House Apprenticeship Program from 1927 – 1930 and was not teaching at Rye during the years Windom references in his memoir (1928 – 1930).

Doing additional research, neither Rye Country Day School nor William Windom historian Jenna Terranova-Frisby could prove the validity of the tale.

Actor William Windom **was NOT** a student of Margaret Hamilton

Back in the Classroom

Margaret cherished the opportunity of portraying a teacher in 1949's *The Red Pony* as she applied her Wheelock training and personal experiences from the kindergarten classroom. But, in an interview years later, when asked if there was any role she played that compared to the mean Wicked Witch of the West, she paused and then said, "I can't think of many parts where I've been truly nasty outside of *Wizard*. Wait a minute! The teacher in *The Red Pony* was very bitchy."

Years later, Margaret's last role, ironically, would be that of a schoolteacher. She was Miss Holderness, a stern 1930s schoolteacher in the September 1982 HBO story *Pardon Me for Living*. In the show, a student presents Miss Holderness with a petition to reduce the amount of geography homework they are being asked to do. In a tone reminiscent of Miss Gulch, she admonishes the student by standing up, leaning forward, and harshly exclaiming to her face, "Shame on you!" followed by an angry statement to the class, "Emily and I *have some business to transact* in Mr. Colby's (the principal) office!"

Margaret Hamilton, in her last role as teacher Miss Holderness in *Pardon Me for Living*

3
CLEVELAND PLAY HOUSE APPRENTICE

Margaret's initial exposure to acting came at an early age. "I was six when the acting bug first hit me. I was the only girl with curls – my mother put my hair up in rags. We had a little club, and to raise money, we put on a play called *Sleeping Beauty*. I had the curls, so I got the part."

Beginning with a small amateur role at The Cleveland Play House as a teenager in 1918 and later playing Sir

Peter Antrobus in the senior play *Pomander Walk* at Hathaway Brown School in 1921, her interest in the theater grew. She explained to *Cleveland Plain Dealer* writer William Hickey in 1973 that her attraction to acting "was no sudden impulse, but rather a building compulsion over the years. I wanted to act, and once you get the desire, nothing else will suffice."

Margaret's interest in the theater continued at Wheelock Kindergarten Training School, where she played "Jo" in the college's 1923 production of *Little Women*.

Following graduation from Wheelock, Margaret returned home to Cleveland in the fall of 1923, juggling a new career as an assistant kindergarten teacher, along with devoting time as a volunteer with the Cleveland Junior League (women's service organization).

Her initial experience as a kindergarten assistant didn't quite go as she imagined. "I was filled with all these wonderful ideas of how to work with children, but I ended up taking off and putting on children's coats and hats and blowing their noses."

The monotony of her role in the kindergarten classroom helped rekindle Margaret's desire to perform on stage – and she did not have far to look while researching local theatrical opportunities.

Located a few blocks away from the Hamilton household, The Cleveland Play House beckoned to Margaret. The Cleveland Play House, established in 1915, developed into one of the country's most renowned theaters and has remained a top Midwest regional theater since its founding over a century ago.

The newly established Cleveland Play House could not have come along at a better time for Margaret. Originating from modest beginnings, the initial Cleveland Play House production in 1916 happened in the attic of a vacant home provided by a generous benefactor. In 1917, Cleveland philanthropists aided The Cleveland Play House by acquiring and renovating a small Lutheran church at the intersection of Cedar and East 73rd Street.

Original Cleveland Play House Cedar and East 73rd Street

Like other small theaters emerging nationwide, people primarily viewed The Cleveland Play House as a local "theater club," and it heavily relied on its members for support. During these formative years, The Cleveland Play House was "an amateur organization wherein the principal benefit accrued to the active participants through their enjoyment of acting, scene-building, and so forth."

A 1919 article in *Cleveland Topics* both praised and poked fun at the newcomer to the Cleveland theatrical scene. Though the article's headline proclaimed, "Art Ability Runs High at Little Theater," the story described how few, if any, local Clevelanders even knew of the theater's existence, quoting a nearby resident who exclaimed, "Well, I'll be –, say, I live right next door to that place and I've been wondering what was going on in that church every night until midnight."

During these early years of The Cleveland Play House, Margaret made her amateur stage debut at the age of 16 in the May 1918 medieval morality play *Everyman*. The play was promoted as being "probably the first production of this old morality in which the stage setting and the costumes will be symbolic rather than realistic." According to the press release, "The production is the most pretentious yet undertaken by the Playhouse group and has been in preparation for several weeks." The article listed out the cast, and for the first time, Margaret Hamilton is credited as being an actress, playing the role of "Discretion" in what would be a lengthy career stretching seven decades.

1918 *Everyman* poster

Play House to Give Morality

The oldest "problem" play in the English language, "Everyman," a play that was the greatest popular success of its day, 430 years ago, will be presented at the Play House, Cedar avenue S. E. and E. 73d street, Friday, Saturday and Sunday evenings.

This morality was written before Columbus discovered America, but though its dramatic quality has kept it alive for over four centuries, the name of its author has passed out of the memory of mankind.

In the production of "Everyman" at the Play House this week there will be a distinct departure in the setting and costuming of the play.

Instead of following the example of other revivals of "Everyman," and attempting to reproduce the crude scenery and the historic costumes of 400 years ago, this most ancient of plays will be staged symbolically and in the most modern manner.

The costumes and stage setting have been designed by William Sommer, the Cleveland artist, known as a devotee of the modern movements in art.

During the presentation of "Everyman" there will be a musical background of improvization on the organ by Charles De Harrack.

The cast includes: Everyman, Judge William Keough; Death, Ben Levin; Fellowship, Albert Hinger; Cousin, Rose Graber; Kindred, Ruth Feather; Goods, Sadie Addo; Good Deeds, Helen Album; Strength, Harry Kurtz; Discretion, Margaret Hamilton; Beauty, Ruth Hopkinson; Five Wits, Ethel Levy; Knowledge, Katherine Kelly; Confession, C. O. Drake.

Margaret Hamiton's amateur stage debut in May 1918 in *Everyman*

The transformation of The Cleveland Play House from a tiny amateurish community theater to a more professional one occurred in 1921. New director Frederic McConnell instituted sweeping changes to make The Cleveland Play House a better-run organization that would serve the larger Cleveland community. Under McConnell's leadership, more performances were added to each theatrical season, along with the hiring of more paid staff.

In 1922, during this dynamic period of growth, the organization introduced an apprentice program that would ultimately benefit Margaret.

Still an amateur actress, Margaret's next Cleveland Play House appearance was several years later in *The Man Who Ate the Popomack* as Lady Phaoron in 1924. The tragicomedy was about a man who ate an exotic fruit, causing him to reek horribly.

Reflecting on *The Man Who Ate the Popomack,* then Cleveland Play House Director Frederic McConnell mused that "for the first time on The Play House stage, a woman smoked a cigar. This was Margaret Hamilton playing none other than Amy Lowell (a cigar-smoking proponent of the times who rebelled against her distinguished Boston lineage)."

Margaret noted later that she didn't know how to smoke before taking the role, and her father refused when she asked him to teach her. She later had to learn from a friend's father.

Her Popomack role would once again whet her appetite for the stage, but teaching and social obligations deferred her acting career for the next few years.

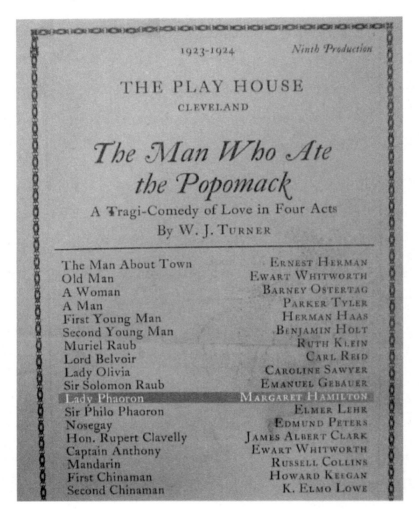

Playbill from *The Man Who Ate the Popomack*

Torn between a teaching career and a continuing fascination with the theater, Margaret accepted a kindergarten teaching position in 1926 at Rye Country Day School in New York to be near the Broadway stage.

After seeing Gertrude Lawrence in the 1926 Broadway musical *Oh Kay!* at the Imperial Theater, Margaret confided that "I was practically crying when I left the theater."

Seeing *Oh Kay!* represented a major milestone in Margaret's life, reaffirming her commitment to pursue acting.

Actress Gertrude Lawrence – star of *Oh Kay!*

Returning home in the summer of 1927 to care for her ailing father, Margaret was once again torn between acting and teaching. To fulfill both aspirations, she found a compromise by teaching nursery school in the morning to allow sufficient time for the rest of the day to pursue her acting dreams.

During the 1920s, The Cleveland Play House experienced a period of tremendous growth and, in 1927, moved into a "new" larger setting on East 86th and Euclid. Housed within the complex were two world-class theaters – the 522-seat Drury Theatre and the smaller, more intimate Brooks Theatre, which housed 160 patrons. With its apprentice development efforts, a Play House School of Theatre opened in 1927 for students from colleges, dramatic schools, and the professional stage. Margaret successfully applied for and was granted acceptance into the program, where she served a three-year apprenticeship from 1927 to 1930.

The "new" Cleveland Play House Drury
Theatre at East 86th and Euclid circa 1927

Looking back at her Cleveland Play House experiences with *Cleveland Plain Dealer* reporter Nan Barnhouse during a trip to Cleveland in 1967, Margaret stated, "I should have had my feet firmly planted on the ground (at age 25), but I would have swept floors if necessary to stay at the Play House."

Margaret would appear in 25 productions while learning her craft at The Cleveland Play House between 1927 and 1930. The atmosphere of the "new" Cleveland Play House of 1927 differed vastly from that of earlier years. Besides the two innovative, top-notch theaters housed within The

Cleveland Play House complex, the dynamic of the theater and its performers had changed from that of a small amateur setting and troupe to that of a self-sustaining professional organization with wide community appeal.

Her apprenticeship began rather modestly. Her first role of the season in November was a tiny part in *The Brothers Karamazov*. She was listed along with 20 other actors under the heading of "Monks, peasants, musicians, soldiers, and dancers." Appearing in a half dozen productions during the 1927 – 1928 season, she slowly gained experience in a more professional environment.

She reiterated the value of working with such professionals as an apprentice while at The Cleveland Play House, sharing a story of how she lost a slipper coming down a flight of stairs, broke up, and started to laugh. Arriving at the bottom of the stairs, one of the veteran professionals in the cast (Carl Benton Reid) scolded her by firmly stating, "If you don't learn to concentrate, you'd better get out right now!" She added, "I've never had any trouble breaking up during a scene since that day."

Ironically, one of Margaret's earliest performances during her Play House apprenticeship was that of playing a witch during the 1927 – 1928 season. She told *Cleveland Plain Dealer* writer Peter Bellamy in 1978 that "I was the First Witch among the Three Witches in *Macbeth*. I never had any idea of playing another witch, although I had loved *The Wizard of Oz* as a little girl and talked about it while teaching kindergarten."

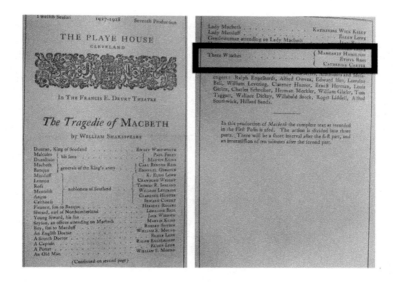

1927 *Macbeth* playbill (right) listing
Margaret Hamilton as one of the production's witches

Other Cleveland Play House productions Margaret appeared in during the 1927 – 1928 season included *Great God Brown* (she played "the mother"), *Anne Pedersdotter* (playing Bente), *The Good Hope* (playing Saart), and *The Tragical History of Doctor Faustus* (appearing as Envy).

[71]

Margaret's theatrical career blossomed after performing several diverse roles in her first full season as a Cleveland Play House apprentice.

The 1928 – 1929 Cleveland Play House season was special for Margaret as she quickly rose in prominence and became a featured Cleveland Play House performer. Previews of upcoming Cleveland Play House productions often featured a publicity photo of Margaret accompanying the article. One of Margaret's earliest publicity photos in the Cleveland newspapers featured her as the sultry Miss Proserpine Garnett in *Candida*.

Margaret Hamilton in *Candida*

Recognized for her artistry in *Candida* and other Play House productions that season, Margaret received many accolades in the press: "This waning theatrical season should not pass into history without some mention of the excellent sequence of performances given by Margaret Hamilton at the Play House. Here is an actress! There are extremely few individuals gifted with as true a sense of comedy as Miss Hamilton possesses. She has a deft and sure touch. She can draw a caricature with bold, broad strokes, or she can, with all finesse and subtlety, paint an arresting portrait. She can be comic and cerebral at the same time. She has a real genius for characterization. On two occasions, she has drawn hearty laughs from a hard-boiled professional of our acquaintance who ordinarily sits through a performance with a face as immovable as an Aztec image when the customers on all sides are suffering from acute giggling hysterics. Good comediennes are rare indeed. Miss Hamilton belongs in this far-from-crowded class."

Additional highlights of the 1928 – 1929 Play House season for Margaret included her role as Erda Leyburn in the highly popular show *The Constant Nymph*, which had an extended performance run. She also received excellent reviews in her highly acclaimed role as governess Charlotte Ivanova in *The Cherry Orchard*. Another key performance for Margaret was that of a Maiden Lady of a Certain Age in *Fashion*. Other roles that season included Kitty Mulberry in *The Texas Nightingale*, the mother in children's drama *The Rusty Hoe* (Jack and the Beanstalk), and a role in *Outside Looking In*.

Publicity photo for *The Cherry Orchard*

Margaret Hamilton in the 1928 Cleveland Play House production of *Fashion*

THE JUNIOR LEAGUE OF CLEVELAND, INC.
Women building better communities

Besides her Cleveland Play House apprenticeship and teaching duties in the late 1920s, Margaret was a very active member of The Junior League of Cleveland, following in the footsteps of her older sisters Gladys and Dorothy.

The Junior League of Cleveland describes itself as "A group of women volunteers dedicated to community change. The group is composed of diverse, creative, compassionate, and action-oriented women who are committed to promoting the League's mission of promoting volunteerism, developing the potential of women, and improving the community through the effective action of trained volunteers."

Margaret very much enjoyed the community service aspect of The Junior League. One of the organization's favorite activities was banding together as The Junior League Players to put on several children's plays (typically over the holidays) with The Cleveland Play House. Coincidentally, one play The Junior League Players performed for children at The Cleveland Play House in 1927 and 1930 was none other than *The Wizard of Oz*. As she helped organize the staging of Oz on behalf of The Junior League, once again, Margaret had no idea of her later life-changing association with the drama.

A "huge venture" of The Junior League Players in May 1929 was staging the revue *Stepping Out* with downtown Cleveland's Hermit Club. Performed at Cleveland's Hanna Theater (instead of the usual Cleveland Play House setting due to scheduling conflicts), *Stepping Out* featured members of both The Junior League Players and Hermit Club. Inspired by Margaret's role in helping to pull off this week-long extravaganza, the local press noted, "As for Miss Hamilton, her talents lie in all directions: acting, singing, radio announcing, and comedy. Hardly a committee that doesn't want her on it, and she too manages to have time for them all."

Tapping Margaret's emerging comedic skills, *Stepping Out* featured her in three humorous skits that were among the revue's highlights. She shone in "If Men

Bought Hats as Women Do," "A New Kind of Rhythm," and "A Ballet Master's Idea of a Drama." As a primary organizer of the event and one of the few professionally trained actresses in the revue, Margaret was a huge reason for the success of *Stepping Out*.

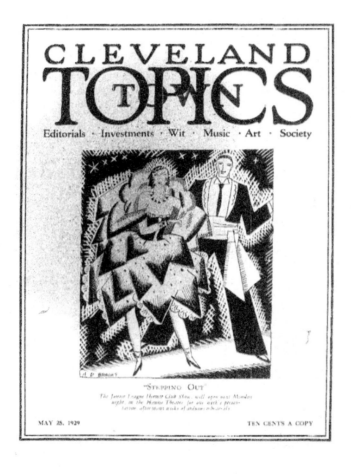

Cleveland Topics cover featuring
The Junior League Players' *Stepping Out*

The Junior League Players' performances for children included an October 1929 presentation of the Grimm Brothers fairy tale classic *The Goose Girl* at The Cleveland Play House, in which Margaret Hamilton played the jester Fustian.

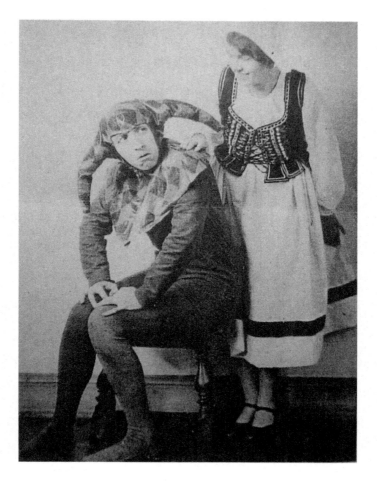

Margaret in The Junior League Players show *The Goose Girl*

Building on her many successful performances, Margaret entered the 1929 – 1930 season as a featured performer at The Cleveland Play House. Despite being classified as an amateur in the Play House's apprenticeship program, Margaret had firmly established herself as a future star in the Cleveland theatrical scene.

In The Cleveland Play House's fourteenth season opener, Margaret played the prominent role of Donna Livia Palegori in the Italian comedy *Each in His Own Way*.

Touted as "an amusing play with something to chew on" by Cleveland theater critic George Davis, *Each in His Own Way* was one of the more challenging efforts ever staged by The Cleveland Play House. Produced for the first time in America, the play was based on a newspaper love scandal and a unique twist in that people who figured in the real-life drama were in the audience seeing the play presented – kind of a play within a play. Newspapers recognized Margaret's contribution to the drama/comedy by mentioning her as both a cast member and a member of the Cleveland Junior League, showing her rising popularity in Cleveland.

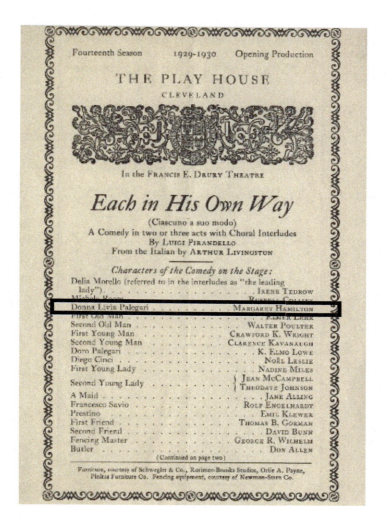

Another highlight of the 1929 – 1930 Cleveland Play House season for Margaret was the presentation of Oscar Wilde's comedy *The Importance of Being Earnest*. Billed as a "trivial comedy for serious people," the play was a sketch of suave London society in the elegant 1890s.

Margaret played Miss Prism, a proper yet tart governess role that tapped her acerbic comic talents once again.

Spurred on by her continued success in many Cleveland Play House presentations, Margaret put together her own vaudeville song and comedy act in late 1929, entitled *Heartrending and Humorous Songs of 1840, 1890, and 1929.*

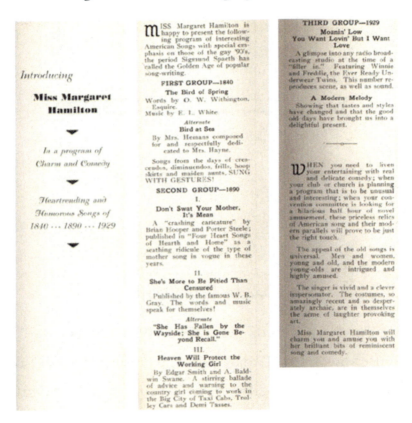

Program from Heartrending and Humorous Songs of 1840, 1890, and 1929

The show debuted at The Cleveland Play House's Brooks Theatre on December 10, 1929, and received a warm reception from the local audience. A *Cleveland Plain Dealer* review of her show the next day proclaimed, "Margaret Hamilton couldn't have suspected the extent of her loyal following, or she would have rented Masonic Hall for her song recital that was given in the much too small Charles Brooks Theatre of the Play House Monday night."

Margaret Hamilton prepares to
sing "Oh Fickle Bird" from her vaudeville show

As Margaret was concluding her triumphant three-year apprenticeship in the spring of 1930, The Cleveland Play House launched a new venture with the noted Chautauqua Institution in southwestern New York.

Margaret and select members of the Play House troupe would reprise five of their most successful productions for the Chautauqua summer theater patrons in July and August:

>*The Importance of Being Earnest*
>
>*Sun-Up*
>
>*Beyond the Horizon*
>
>*Candida*
>
>*The Mollusc*

Chautauqua Institution – 1930
Summer Home for The Cleveland Play House

For the first time in her career, Margaret was paid for her performances in Chautauqua's summer stock productions. "It was the first time I was ever paid for acting – $50 a week," Margaret noted some years later. With her days as an amateur actress now officially over, Margaret set her sights on a professional acting career.

Being paid as a professional actress during her summer stock performances at Chautauqua in 1930 fueled Margaret's determination to make acting her career. Following that, Margaret got a part in the musical comedy *Ship Shapes* (*The Cape Cod Follies*) at the Cape Playhouse in Dennis, Massachusetts, in late August 1930.

The Cape Playhouse in Dennis, Massachusetts

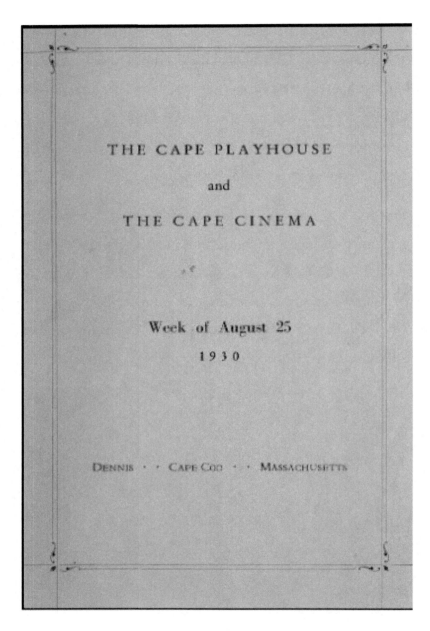

Playbill for The Cape Playhouse
with *Ship Shapes* featuring Margaret Hamilton

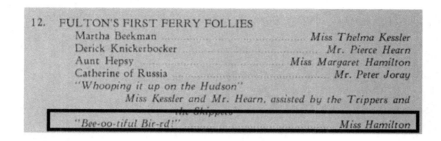

Margaret got a chance to sing several songs in *Ship Shapes,* including "Bee-oo-tiful Bir-rd!"

PART TWO	
1. THE FLEET AND THE FLIRTS OF THE NINETIES	
Miss Diploma	Miss Thelma Kessler
Lieutenant	Mr. Pierce Hearn
The Sweet-heart of the Fleet	Miss Margaret Hamilton
Little Buttercup	Miss Peggy Ellis
Sir Joseph Porter, K. C. B.	Mr. Bradley Cass
Dick Dead-eye	Mr. L'Estrange Millman
Her Majesty	Mr. Peter Joray
The Trippers and The Skippers	
"When Souza Sent The Navy Off To War"	Miss Hamilton
"That Cabaret Revue"	Miss Ellis, Miss Hamilton, and Mr. Cass

Margaret appeared as "The Sweet-heart of the Fleet"
in one of the acts in *Ship Shapes*

Encouraged by the success of obtaining an acting role outside of her Cleveland Play House roots, Margaret set her sights on the bright lights of Broadway.

Margaret's timing to become a Broadway actress could not have been worse.

[87]

As the Great Depression cast a shadow over America in late 1929, the theater world felt its chilling effects. For Margaret, the dream of Broadway seemed more distant than ever. The bustling stages she longed to be a part of were now plagued by financial uncertainty and dwindling audiences.

The Broadway season from 1929 to 1930 was not heavily impacted by the Depression thanks to pre-purchased subscription packages, maintaining somewhat normal attendance. However, the impact of the Great Depression significantly affected the Broadway season of 1930-1931.

1929's Great Depression affected all
aspects of American life, including Broadway

The winter of 1930/31 was quite humbling for Margaret. The combination of being a "new" professional actress, coupled with competing against a surplus of experienced actresses for far fewer theatrical roles (because of The Great Depression), would make landing any kind of Broadway part a major challenge for Margaret.

Living off the $100 a month that her father provided, Margaret noted, "I would make the rounds of all the theatrical agencies every day and auditioned for whatever production I heard about. At least making the rounds salves the soul and gives you the feeling you are in show business."

She stated her conversations with the New York theater managers were brief and to the point. "They would ask, 'What is your experience?' Well, I acted in the Play House of Cleveland – 'Oh, an amateur. No use coming to us until you've had some New York experience!'"

"I got absolutely nowhere and was so disheartened that I nearly despaired of ever getting a chance to do anything." For a while, it appeared Margaret would never make her magical journey to Oz.

4
LIONS AND TIGERS AND BROADWAY (OH MY!)

The summer of 1931 would fare much better for Margaret after months of trying to land an acting position.

She met landscape architect Paul Boynton Meserve from New York earlier while he was in Cleveland working on a project, and the couple became engaged. News of Margaret's upcoming nuptials, marriage, and honeymoon all made Cleveland's society pages.

The groom, Paul Boynton Meserve, was originally from Framingham, Massachusetts, where he grew up and graduated from high school. He later received his college degree in architecture from the prestigious Cornell University in 1925.

 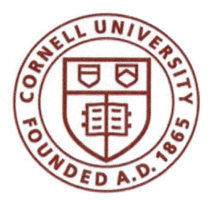

Paul Boynton Meserve

On June 13, 1931, they were married, and Margaret "wore a gown of pearl satin, a close-fitting model with train cut in the skirt, and long tight sleeves." The matron of honor was Margaret's older sister, Gladys, while the maid of honor was her cousin, Martha Adams.

Margaret Hamilton with her sister
and matron of honor, Gladys Mohler

The wedding took place at Calvary Presbyterian Church in Cleveland, and hundreds of guests were in attendance. The reception was held at the prestigious Shaker Tavern on Shaker Square. The local press provided a comprehensive account of the wedding's details.

Calvary Presbyterian Church is one of the few sites associated with Margaret's early Cleveland years that still exists. The church was one of the few buildings damaged in a Cleveland tornado in 2023 when a good portion of its roof blew off. Quite the irony, given the key role a tornado played in *The Wizard of Oz*.

Calvary Presbyterian Church at East 79th and Euclid was the site of Margaret's wedding

Following a Bermuda honeymoon, the Meserves took up residence in New York City, which would ultimately benefit Margaret's Broadway dreams.

In the summer of 1931, encouraged by her new husband, Margaret refocused her thespian ambitions back to summer stock based on the previous summer's positive Chautauqua experience. Though still somewhat disappointed by her failed Broadway casting calls, Margaret hoped that by doing summer stock again, she'd continue developing her acting skills as she sought her lucky break in show business.

Margaret's idea to pursue summer stock again in 1931 was a wise decision. A choice that would, after a year's anxious delay, lead to her big show business break.

It just so happened that aspiring director/producer Arthur J. Beckhard was crafting several new summer stock try-out plays in 1931 at the Greenwich Civic Theatre in Connecticut, hoping one of his productions might be worthy of being produced later on Broadway.

Following her honeymoon, Margaret reunited with an old friend and former Cleveland Play House alumnus, Ellen Lowe (the sister of The Cleveland Play House's actor K. Elmo Lowe), and the two actresses were invited by Arthur Beckhard to be in the cast of his play *Metronome*, which was one of the Greenwich summer try-out plays he organized.

Margaret described in a 1982 Cinekyd cable access television interview how she already knew Beckhard, who called her stating, "they needed an older lady to play this part" and asked, "Maggie, I wish you would come play this part." When Beckhard added that even though there was already a young girl slated for the part, she was too young for the role and would get a much nicer part. Margaret was initially reluctant to replace her. After assurances from Beckhard, Margaret told him, "Well, all right, I'd love to," noting, "I played her part, then I played another and another and another" that summer after replacing Marjorie Anderson as Mrs. Birch in *Metronome*.

THE NEW PLAY

METRONOME, a new play by Arthur J. Beckhard, presented at the Greenwich Civic Theater. Staged by the author. The Cast:

Mrs. Sarah Dickinson	Ellen Lowe
Abby Minot	Ellen Back
Millie Pease	Helen Hale
Mrs. Will Hatch	Bertha Boles
Martha	Katherine Squire
Dr. Will Hatch	Benjamin Trask Kiley
Stephen Wroblowski	Byron McGrath
Philip	Enzo Aita
Elizabeth-Ann Dickinson	Ruth Garland
Judson Beasley	Barry Mahool
Bob Dickinson	Bruce MacFarlane
Dickie Robert	Richard Beckhard
Mamie Beaseley	Helen Robinson
Alice	Marjorie Anderson
Mrs. Elder	Rita Rheinfrank
Mrs. Birch	Marjorie Anderson
Madame Dolores Bellini	Esther Dale

Metronome play in which Margaret would replace Marjorie Anderson as Mrs. Birch

---

GREENWICH CIVIC THEATRE
(Direction: Arthur J. Beckhard)
GREENWICH, CONN.

This Week "METRONOME"
A new play by Arthur J. Beckhard with
ESTHER DALE and RUTH GARLAND

Week Beginning August 3
"ECHO"
A new play by Leila Manning Taylor
EVENINGS AT 8:50 —— NO MATINEES
Prices: Orchestra by Subscription $1.00 to $2.00
Single Performances $1.50 to $3.00 —— Entire Balcony 50c
Box Office Telephones GREENWICH 3502, 3503

July 1931 ad for *Metronome*

Margaret's performance in *Metronome* was impressive enough for the local *Greenwich News and Graphic* newspaper to note, "Miss Margaret Hamilton, who scored a distinct personal success as Mrs. Birch in *Metronome,* will give a program of character songs and characterizations at the Greenwich Theatre on Sunday evening, August 2, 1931." Margaret's August 2nd program was a reprise of her comedic vaudeville show that she'd performed at The Cleveland Play House in late 1929.

Margaret followed her August 2nd vaudeville show with a mid-August Greenwich summer stock role in the comedy *I Knew Him When.* *The Greenwich News* review reported Hamilton was "perfect" as Mrs. Vail.

[97]

As the 1931 Greenwich summer stock season was winding down, Arthur Beckhard cast Margaret in late August's production of *Hallam Wives* following her string of successful performances. As it turned out, *Hallam Wives* would be the show that ultimately jump-started Margaret's stage and, in turn, movie career.

August 1931 ad for *Hallam Wives* that
Margaret appeared in, leading to her "big break"

Hallam Wives was described as a family drama in which bickering in-laws clash amusingly with one another under the dominance of the Hallam family's matriarch. The play provided the opportunity for lively dialogue and plenty of laughs – especially for Margaret's role.

[98]

After her week-long late summer performance in *Hallam Wives*, Margaret thought her acting career was over. She was ready to accept a teaching position in Pennsylvania.

Just one day before accepting the teaching offer, she got the news that *Hallam Wives* was going to head to Broadway in 1933, and her career was launched.

Hallam Wives underwent a name change to *Another Language* before making its way to Broadway's Booth Theatre on April 25, 1932. After a successful two-week stint in Washington, D.C., Margaret played the role of sarcastic daughter-in-law, Helen Hallam, in the play.

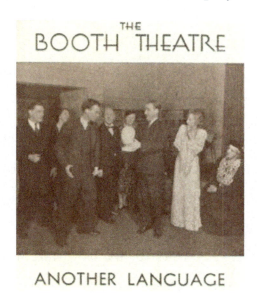

Playbill for *Another Language* (Margaret is by the doorway)

Another Language became a surprise hit on Broadway in 1932, drew rave reviews, and went for a run of 344 performances. *The New York Times* review of *Another Language* stated that "although *Another Language* is the first play by Rose Franken to reach Broadway, it is a singularly complete revelation of character and a remarkably workmanlike achievement. Here is one play that belongs to the theater." The review noted that "Margaret Hamilton finds the acid humor in Helen's resigned view of the world."

Accolades for Margaret (through her performance as Helen Hallam) quickly stacked up. *The New York Herald Tribune* recognized her as one of Broadway's top impersonators, and she received similar praise from the *World Telegram, Vanity Fair,* and *The New Yorker*.

"The critics were very kind to me. Their reviews brought me to the attention of other Broadway producers and Hollywood types, and my career was launched," Margaret noted. She also took delight in pointing out how most of the reviews referred to her as "Margaret Hamilton from the provinces."

When asked how she felt the first time the curtain went up on her Broadway debut, Margaret offered the following insight: "Well, just before I went on, it came over me with a rush that this was actually New York, and I had *arrived,* but once I was on the stage, I became Helen Hallam and forgot all about the audience."

Margaret Hamilton in *Another Language*

"So, you see, it was just luck after all, and I shall never cease to be grateful to Arthur Beckhard for giving me my chance," noted Margaret in a 1933 *Bystander* interview.

She echoed these same sentiments again some 40 years later in 1973 to *Cleveland Plain Dealer* writer William Hickey, saying, "The history of the theater is rife with stories about this, and that person being discovered while performing in a very minor part. It happened to me (referring to her role in Arthur Beckhard's breakthrough role in *Hallam Wives*). It has happened to the biggest names in our profession."

Margaret found success in Hollywood when *Another Language* was adapted into a film, but she remained passionate about theater.

"The theater is such a full, complete experience as opposed to the lack of it in movies, in which you have to build a character instantly. The stage is a little like playing golf. If you have a bad day, there's always the opportunity to analyze your shortcomings and then go back the next day and try to do it better. Only in the theater do you have the opportunity to experiment, to change, to grow, and to improve each performance. In no other acting medium is there such freedom of movement and complete control. And then, of course, there is the immediate response of the audience – vital and inviting. You literally 'feel' the audience. This is why one can play a part for a year and feel excited each night when the curtain goes up."

Interestingly, friend and former Cleveland Play House alum Ellen E. Lowe (noted earlier) would also end up playing Helen Hallam with the touring troupe of *Another Language*.

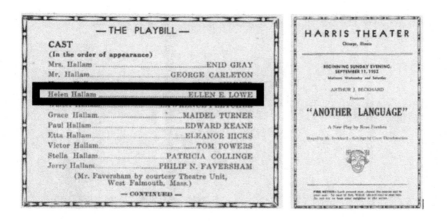

Playbill noting Margaret's friend Ellen E. Lowe as Helen Hallam

Another coincidence for Margaret, looking back to the original 1931 "try-out" of *Hallam Wives* (before *Another Language*), was crossing paths with the star of the play - Maria Ouspenkaya. Maria was both a brilliant Russian stage and film actress, besides being a legendary acting teacher.

Margaret would go on to attend Maria's acting school, which focused on "method" acting.

Through training, she learned to use her physical, mental, and emotional self to bring a character to life, which became one of her greatest strengths.

Margaret's teacher as a gypsy in 1941's *The Wolf Man*

Taking advantage of her quick rise to theatrical fame on Broadway, Margaret decided to restage her highly successful one-woman play that she had done three years earlier back home in Cleveland. Staged at the Booth Theatre in June 1932, where *Another Language* was in the midst of its successful year-long run, Margaret's show provided another opportunity to showcase her many diverse talents.

Ironically, one of the newspaper advertisements for her show was right above that of a competing Broadway show starring Frank Morgan – none other than the Wizard himself!

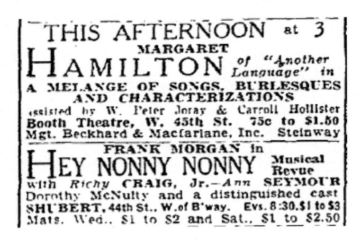

Ad for Margaret's Broadway show
above that of Frank Morgan (the Wizard in Oz)

In New York in 1932, Margaret's vaudeville comedy and song show did not receive the same level of acclaim as it did in Cleveland in 1929. Despite receiving mixed reviews, Margaret's own show helped her gain more recognition in New York's theater scene.

MARGARET HAMILTON MAKES RECITAL DEBUT

Actress of "Another Language" Company Presents Program at the Booth Theatre.

At the Booth Theatre, where the bickering House of Hallam assembles nightly in "Another Language," Margaret Hamilton, the acidulous Helen of that clan, made her first New York recital appearance yesterday afternoon.

It was in another mood and in other guises that Miss Hamilton left Helen Hallam behind her—a mood limited entirely to burlesque, frequently a little forced and steadily lacking in variety until her final number. For three of her four portraits were of the lady who, to paraphrase Bobby Clark's now immortal phrase, "Don't sing good, but sings loud."

As an eloping girl of the '40s, a "guest artist" or a prima donna, Miss Hamilton kept, song for song, essentially the same character and the same blunt methods. It would be risking boredom if attempted even by Beatrice Lillie, who specializes in these matters. Only in her concluding sketch, as the announcer, singer and speaker on a radio hour, did Miss Hamilton yield to the variety which might well have marked her program as a whole. Successful as she was in that finale—for her humor is real though obvious—it was, nevertheless, the finale and, naturally, somewhat too late.

Following a year-long successful run in *Another Language*, Margaret's next Broadway appearance was in the November 1933 mystery drama *The Dark Tower*. Advertised as a blend of murder and mystery, *The Dark Tower* was poorly received by theater critics in New York and had a brief run at the Morosco Theatre. Margaret played the "acidulous spinster Hattie," providing a preview of the many spinster roles she would come to play in her lengthy career as an actress.

As *The Dark Tower* was closing, Margaret received great news. *Another Language* had been such a hit on Broadway that Hollywood wanted to make the play into a movie.

The movie version of the Broadway show features Margaret and two other actors reprising their roles. In just a few years, Margaret went from struggling to find work on Broadway to becoming a part of a hit show and soon-to-be Hollywood actress, getting closer to Oz.

Margaret's third Broadway appearance was in 1934's *The Farmer Takes a Wife*. The play was remarkable for multiple reasons, notably Henry Fonda's first major role on Broadway and the subsequent movie adaptation with Fonda and Hamilton reprising their stage characters. Margaret would appear in five films with her friend "Hank" over the years.

The New York Times review noted, "As Dan Harrow, Henry Fonda, who has his first big opportunity here, gives a manly, modest performance in a style of captivating simplicity." The same review was also complimentary in noting that "Although Margaret Hamilton lacks the poundage of the original Lucy Gurget, her sense of humor is up to the part."

Margaret, Henry Fonda, and Janet Gaynor
in *The Farmer Takes a Wife*

In the 1969 Broadway revival of *Our Town*, Margaret had the chance to play Mrs. Soames with Henry Fonda, her old friend from their first Broadway performance together 35 years earlier. *Our Town* was Margaret's last play on Broadway (she later did a few touring Broadway shows).

5

I HAVE A FEELING WE'RE NOT IN KANSAS ANYMORE!

The unexpected Broadway success of *Another Language*, both popularly and critically, led to the play being turned into a movie in 1933. Margaret Hamilton was requested to once again play the role of Helen Hallam, the sharp-tongued aunt known for her insatiable grape-eating habits.

Another Language, Margaret Hamilton's first movie

Margaret (third for the left) as Helen Hallam in *Another Language*

Following the filming of *Another Language* in 1933, Margaret returned to Broadway for two more plays – *The Dark Tower*, which went from November 1933 through January 1934, and later, *The Farmer Takes a Wife*, which ran from October 1934 through January 1935.

Sandwiched in between her 1934 Broadway productions, Margaret would travel to Hollywood in 1934, signing a one-year deal with RKO Studios to knock out four quick summer movie roles as a budding character actress. The movies were: *Broadway Bill, By Your Leave, There's Always Tomorrow,* and *Hat, Coat, and Glove.*

Having now appeared in several films and having established herself as a successful character actress, Margaret and her husband Paul would choose to move to California in 1935 from New York. Just before the move to California, where she would remain for the next 15 years, the long hours associated with her acting career and frequent trips back and forth between a stage career in New York City and movie roles in Hollywood began to put a strain on her marriage.

Shortly after settling down in California, Margaret experienced several life-changing events during the next few years. On August 22, 1935, her father passed away in Cleveland. W.J. Hamilton's estate, valued at $400,000 (equivalent to 9 million dollars today), was left without a will following his death. The probate court then distributed the estate among Margaret and her three siblings, with each expected to inherit around the equivalent of 2 million dollars in late 1935.

W. J. HAMILTON, ATTORNEY, DEAD

Judge's Son, 45 Years a Lawyer Here, Was Known as One of Ablest.

Walter J. Hamilton, 70, for 45 years an active member of the Cleveland bar and considered by his fellow attorneys as one of the ablest died yesterday at Lakeside Hospital after a short illness.

Born in Cuyahoga County, he was the son of Edwin T. Hamilton, 30 consecutive years a judge in the Common Pleas Court. His mother was a sister of William S. Jones, one of the earlier presidents of the Society for Savings.

Mr. Hamilton was a graduate of the University of Michigan, where he won his A. B., and Cornell University, where he was graduated in law. He was best known as a counselor and rarely participated in trial or court work.

His wife, who died several years ago, was a sister of the late Charles E. Adams.

Mr. Hamilton was of a retiring nature and did not belong to social clubs, but was a member of both the Cleveland and American Bar Associations. As one of his brother lawyers expressed it:

"He realized the law was a jealous mistress and for that reason devoted his time to it."

He is survived by three daughters, Mrs. Margaret H. Meserve of Los Angeles, who as Margaret Hamilton was one of the active members of the Play House group and later achieved distinction on the New York stage; Mrs. Dorothy H. Dick of New York and Mrs. Gladys H. Mohler of Columbus; one son, Edwin T. Hamilton of New York, and a sister, Miss Florence Hamilton.

Mrs. Dick, after the death of her first husband, Charles F. Brush, jr., was active in charitable work, having at one time opened her estate as a playground and camp for children. The son is a well known writer of books on aviation. During the war he served in the British aviation service.

Funeral services will be held at 3:30 tomorrow afternoon at the residence, 2058 E. 96th Street, with private burial.

On June 12, 1936, Margaret gave birth to Hamilton (Ham) Wadsworth Meserve in Los Angeles, five years after they were married. Ham inherited his mother's nickname and ended up being the only child Margaret ever had.

Two years following her son's birth, Margaret's marriage to Paul Meserve ended officially on May 20, 1938. In divorce court, each accused the other of causing the end of the marriage. Paul claimed Margaret was throwing too many wild parties at their home, while she countered he was just after her money and was the victim of spousal abuse.

Since Margaret was a public figure through her growing acting career, the sordid details of her turbulent marriage were splashed across the various local newspapers. Salacious newspaper stories covered the problems they were having, including Margaret's initial divorce request a year earlier in 1937 (which she rescinded) and a lawsuit from their housekeeper alleging Mr. Meserve had attacked her, along with Margaret's complaints of being punched in the face by her husband.

Following the divorce proceedings, Margaret gained custody of young Ham, and they settled down in Beverly Hills, California.

Margaret spoke to *New York Times* reporter Howard Thompson years later about her brief failed marriage. "It simply didn't work out, but we separated on good terms and didn't just hang on. I think that kind of marriage can hurt a growing child. Children are so observant."

Two years after divorcing Margaret, Paul Meserve married Ruth Rakowsky Mayo in July 1940 in Rochester, Minnesota. Ruth was the young widow of Joseph Mayo, a noted surgeon (and son of Mayo Clinic founder Dr. Charles Mayo) who died in a car crash with a train a few years prior.

Mrs. Ruth Mayo of Rochester Wed to Californian

Rochester, Minn. — Simplicity marked the ceremony Wednesday at which Mrs. Ruth Mayo of Rochester became the bride of Paul Boynton Meserve of Rochester, formerly of California.

Dr. O. P. Sheridan read the marriage service in the chapel at the Congregational church in the presence of the immediate family at 11 a. m. Mrs. Hendrik Svien of Rochester, sister of the bride, was her only attendant. Dr. Charles W. Mayo, brother-in-law of the bride, was best man.

Following the ceremony, a small reception was given at the home of the bride, Bird Lodge, at Mayowood. Attending the wedding were the bride's parents, Mr. and Mrs. Victor Rakowsky of Joplin, Mo.

Upon their return from a trip on the Mississippi river to St. Louis, aboard the Blue Wren, Mr. and Mrs. Meserve will reside temporarily in Rochester.

Rochester Woman Dies by Own Hand

Rochester, Minn. —(U.P.)— Mrs. Paul Meserve, widow of Dr. Joseph G. Mayo, died by her own hand here Sunday.

Dr. J. E. Crewe, county coroner, pronounced a verdict of suicide and stated Mrs. Meserve had been in ill health and depressed for some time. No inquest will be held.

Her body was found at her home, Bird Lodge at Mayowood, Mayo family estate near Rochester, at 4:30 a. m.

The coroner said she had fired a pistol bullet into her head.

She is survived by her husband, Paul Meserve of Rochester, and two children by her previous marriage.

Her first husband, Dr. Joseph Graham Mayo, was the son of the late Dr. Charles H. Mayo, co-founder of the Mayo clinic.

[116]

In 1942, two years into their marriage, the new Mrs. Meserve was initially reported to have been "Found Shot to Death" by a local newspaper. Her cause of death was later revised to suicide. Ruth's final resting place is Oakwood Cemetery in Rochester, Minnesota, alongside her first husband, Joseph Mayo. Though officially "Mrs. Ruth Meserve" at the time of her death, no last name is on her grave.

After the tragic end of their marriage, Paul Meserve soon returned to California.

Over the years, Margaret had minimal contact with Paul Meserve, who spent much of his life as a landscape architect and city planner in Sausalito, California.

After her 1938 divorce, Margaret followed an approach of playing primarily maids and housekeepers in movies, along with an occasional spinster or town gossip role. As a single mother, her goal was to maintain steady employment as a character actress. She never asked for more than $1,000 a week. Margaret refused to become a contract player, thus not limiting herself to working for one studio.

Margaret discussed her strategy with friend and author Aljean Harmetz: "At $1,200 or $1,500 a week, I knew I wouldn't work much. And I had my young son, and I wanted to work all I could. So, I never let them pay me more. And I never went under contract. If you looked like me, you got all the parts where you opened the door and said, 'I'm sorry, he's not here, goodbye,' and shut the door. Even so, I got a lot of those parts."

Margaret was also aware of her unique appearance as it related to landing most of her character roles. As a young child, she played Sleeping Beauty, a role that, as she put it, was her "first acting appearance and the last time, if I may say, I ever played a beauty of any kind." Margaret not only accepted her looks, but she embraced them to great advantage.

In *Parade Magazine's* aptly titled "I'm Glad I'm Homely" interview, Margaret confided her father offered to get her a nose job as a child, but she declined the proposal. A lucky turn for her future acting career. She added that during the filming of The Wizard of Oz, "They put a sign on my chair, 'Mag the Hag.' Why, I just loved it. I'm not sensitive about my looks." She'd often add "Mag the Hag" when signing autographs, along with her standard "WWW" signature.

"Mag the Hag!" signature

Years later, in 1959, drawing upon the limited dialogue she often had in her brief maid and housekeeper movie roles, Margaret performed a piece called "Aprons I Have Worn" in her one-woman show *Ham's Hash*, at Moylan, Pennsylvania's Hedgerow Theatre, poking fun at herself.

Margaret Hamilton in *Ham's Hash* performed "Aprons I Have Worn"

Hedgerow Theatre Moylan, Pennsylvania

Despite the life-changing events of the birth of her son in 1936 and subsequent divorce in 1938, Margaret was able to settle down in Beverly Hills and continued to garner steady employment as a character actress. She ended up appearing in over 20 movies before her breakthrough role as the Wicked Witch of the West in 1939's *The Wizard of Oz*.

As a steadily employed actress, beginning early in her lengthy career, Margaret crossed paths with a veritable "who's who" of stars from film and, later, television.

Among those actors, Margaret crossed paths with prior to Oz was the actual wizard himself - Frank Morgan. Margaret and Frank would appear together in three films before making *The Wizard of Oz*, not knowing the celebrity that would await the film's participants years later.

She described Frank Morgan's acting abilities, saying, "He was a very, very, professional player," later adding, "he was very lovable, very sweet, very considerate, and one of the nicest people I knew."

Margaret and Morgan appeared together with Clark Gable in 1937's *Saratoga*, two years before *The Wizard of Oz* and *Gone with the Wind*.

Morgan passed away in 1949, sharing very little in the fame that would come after the movie's annual showings began in the late 1950s.

Margaret and Frank Morgan movies together:

    1934 *By Your Leave*
    1934 *There's Always Tomorrow*
    1937 *Saratoga*

Clark Gable, Jean Harlow, Frank Morgan, and Margaret in *Saratoga*

Margaret would appear early on with many notable Hollywood stars, including some up-and-coming ones before Oz, including Lucille Ball. Both had a brief part (Margaret as Edna) in the 1934 film *Broadway Bill*, with Lucy appearing as a blond telephone operator.

One of Margaret's more humorous roles was that of Beulah Flanders, as a shotgun-toting farm gal widowed five times looking for another husband (victim?) in 1938's *Stablemates*, which included a youthful Mickey Rooney.

The Kansas City Star's review of *Stablemates* stated, "Funniest scene goes to Margaret Hamilton, five times a widow, looking for another victim chooses Beery (actor Wallace Beery playing an alcoholic veterinarian). With only a look, she brings the house down."

And there was no shortage of "star power" when Margaret (as housekeeper Amy) had a small part in *Four's A Crowd* in 1938, featuring Errol Flynn and Olivia de Havilland.

Actors from early movies Margaret was in (clockwise from upper left) Errol Flynn, Lucille Ball, Olivia de Havilland, and Mickey Rooney

Margaret occasionally got the chance to showcase her witty and cantankerous personality in a few movies, going beyond brief dialogues. One of Margaret's most interesting early character roles before her breakthrough Oz characterization of the Wicked Witch was running a General Store in 1937's *Nothing Sacred*. The part would be prophetic of her second most popular career role – store proprietor Cora in the 1970s Maxwell House coffee commercials.

Margaret Hamilton tends to her General Store in *Nothing Sacred*

While Margaret was establishing a strong portfolio of character roles in films, she continued to stay involved with the Los Angeles Junior League alongside her other pursuits.

As circumstances would have it, The Junior League planned to perform *The Wizard of Oz* in 1937 at a couple of local schools in Los Angeles. Margaret, as fate would have it, landed the role of the "Bad Witch of the West."

Filming for the movie version of *The Wizard of Oz* would begin the following year in Hollywood in 1938 – quite a coincidence. Little did Margret realize just where her small role in The Junior League play would/lead her.

6
MAKING A WICKED WITCH

An angry Wicked Witch of the West (Margaret Hamilton) arrives in Munchkinland

Margaret Hamilton's appearance in *The Wizard of Oz* was for a mere 12 minutes of screen time. Her frightening iconic portrayal as the Wicked Witch of the West (while also playing Almira Gulch) landed her in the fourth spot on the American Film Institute's "Top 100 Movie Villains of All Time" list. The Wicked Witch of the West's menacing line **"I'll get you my pretty, and your little dog, too!"** came in at #99 on the American Film Institute's "Top 100 Movie Quotes of All Time."

While not on any list per se, Margaret's delivery of the witch's last lines, "I'm melting, melting. Ohhhhh, what a world, what a world. Who would have thought that some little girl like you could destroy my beautiful wickedness..." also became part of the American vernacular. Margaret herself would later joke in a 1975 *Wilmington News Journal* interview that over the years, she lost four inches in height through slipped disks and quipped, "Maybe I'm melting!"

The song "Ding Dong the Witch is Dead" came in at #82 on the American Film Institute's "Top 100 Songs of Cinema." The song ironically had a renaissance of sorts in 2013, charting to #2 on the UK Singles chart following the death of Margaret Thatcher, former British Prime Minister.

And yet, surprisingly, Margaret Hamilton was not the first choice to play the Wicked Witch of the West in *The Wizard of Oz*!

When creating the movie adaptation of L. Frank Baum's classic 1900 novel *The Wonderful Wizard of Oz*, MGM Studios faced many obstacles. One of the greatest challenges was the casting of the actors to portray the key characters from the beloved tale. This included who would play The Wicked Witch of the West.

The Wonderful Wizard of Oz and the original
Wicked Witch of the West novel depiction

Acclaimed Oz author Bill Stillman shared how the original concept of the Witch for the movie was "that she was a gruff harridan (an unpleasant belligerent old woman). That shifted in the spring of 1938 after (Mervyn) LeRoy screened *Snow White* for his unit." LeRoy's first choice for the part was Academy Award-winning actress Gale Sondergaard. He envisioned Sondergaard wearing a tight-fitting black sequined dress, a black sequined hat, and green eye shadow.

Snow White's wicked queen was the model
for potential Oz film witch Gale Sondergaard

Gale Sondergaard, as a slinky, glamorous witch, was not to be. Shown as a beautiful witch (right) and then recast as a more traditional witch, Gale Sondergaard backed out of the film.

"I said, 'Fine, Mervyn. I really don't want to be an ugly, hateful witch,'" Sondergaard recalled. "And that was the end of it. In those days, I was not about to make myself ugly for any motion picture."

The parting was mutual, and in a 1972 interview, Oz Producer Mervyn LeRoy admitted Gale was "too pretty. We needed somebody who could scare the pants off children."

Enter Margaret Hamilton

Margaret Hamilton recalled over the years at several Oz-related gatherings how she had always adored *The Wizard of Oz,* including a 1979 Topeka event: "I'd had it read to me when I was four years old; my mother bought it for me. But it never occurred to me that I'd ever be the Witch... (*Dorothy*, maybe!) But one day, my agent called and said, 'Maggie, he said, they're really kind of interested in you for a part in *The Wizard of Oz*.' And I said, 'Oh gosh! Think of that! I've loved that story from the time I was four years old! What part is it?' And he said, 'Well...the Witch.' And I said, 'The *Witch*?!' And he said – 'Yes...what else?'"

Thus, while working on the MGM film *Stablemates* in 1938, Margaret Hamilton could cram in a screen test for a chance to play the Wicked Witch of the West in *The Wizard of Oz*.

Margaret recounted in an interview with James Bawden how "she was at a football game with her little son, and Mervyn spotted me and ran over and said, 'We've been looking for you everywhere. You got it! Report Monday for costume and makeup tests.' He offered me six weeks at $1,000 a week, which was manna for me. It eventually stretched out to twenty-three weeks."

One week after Gale Sondergaard's "ugly" tests, the MGM news-of-the-day teletype of October 10, 1938, announced, "Margaret Hamilton replaces Gale Sondergaard in the role of the Wicked Witch of the West."

Various iterations of Margaret Hamilton's Wicked Witch of the West character's look were tested. The photo on the next page from early filming shows Margaret with her hair down, along with different face makeup and fewer prosthetics. In the final version of the film, her hair was tied back in a bun to highlight the witch's face, resulting in a more intense and frightening effect. The definitive terrifying version of the Wicked Witch of the West seen in *The Wizard of Oz* featured a rubber nose, chin, and wart, which had to be glued to Margaret's face, along with having her face, neck, and hands coated with green paint.

Margaret Hamilton in early Wicked Witch of the West "look"

Partway through the filming, Margaret noticed her skin had acquired a green tinge, even when she wasn't in makeup. It was months before her skin was normal again. Green-tinted skin was a mild problem compared to Hamilton's life-threatening accident on the Munchkinland set.

In the scene where the Wicked Witch of the West makes a fiery exit from Munchkinland, Margaret was severely burned. To film the scene, Margaret needed to drop down a small elevator through a hidden trapdoor as the fiery pyrotechnics occurred. The timing was everything, given the danger factor. The first take of the scene was perfect and ultimately used in the film. When they filmed a later retake of the scene (as was standard practice), a terrible accident occurred.

Margaret described the ensuing horrific experience to James Bawden. "I had to drop six feet through a trapdoor with the colored smoke all around me, and it was a close-up, so there was no double. I was told to bend my knees, and I'd land simply, but suddenly I was in flames. Somebody had prematurely touched the fire button. I was on fire! My broomstick went right up! My hat was on fire! I had to be hospitalized (at home) for second-degree burns for over a month."

Oz makeup man Jack Young quickly and carefully wiped off the toxic copper-laden green makeup with alcohol when the accident happened. His quick work helped prevent the toxic makeup from seeping further into her burned skin, where it would have caused a serious infection. She suffered second-degree burns on her face and third-degree burns on one hand. Returning to the set, Margaret had to wear green gloves for the majority of the filming because her nerves were exposed on one hand.

Here's a visualization of the tragic sequence in which Margaret is burned as she exits Munchkinland:

TO PULL OFF HER MUNCHKINLAND EXIT, MARGARET TUCKED IN HER ELBOWS AND HELD THE BROOM UPRIGHT TO FIT ON THE SLIM ELEVATOR PLATFORM AS IT TOOK HER SWIFTLY BELOW THE STAGE.

WHEN REDOING THE SCENE, THE FLAMES WENT OFF TOO SOON AS SHE DESCENDED.

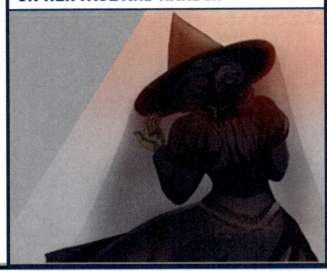
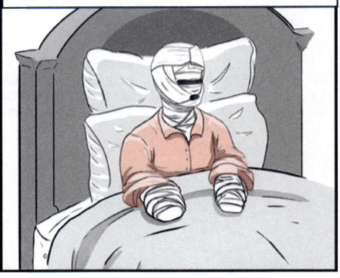

Years after the tragic accident, Margaret's son Hamilton Meserve, shared with *The Topeka Capital-Journal's* Bill Blankenship how, as a three-year-old visiting his mom at the hospital,[2] he was told his mother would "have a wonderful costume on. She looks just like a mummy."

Hamilton remembered his mother's head being fully wrapped in bandages, except for her left eye, yet she still managed to make jokes about her appearance.

Margaret noted that MGM grudgingly paid her attending physician, who monitored her recovery at home. Her agent told her that if she sued, she'd never work in Hollywood again.

When Margaret returned to the set in February, she was asked to do the scene where the witch skywrites "Surrender Dorothy." Margaret recalled, "I was told I'd be suspended in the air with a long pipe emitting smoke below me. I said no, and they said I was a sissy and brought in the stand-in, and she saddled up, and the whole gadget

---

[2] Margaret's son was only two at the time of the accident and she recuperated at home not the hospital, as detailed extensively in *The Making of The Wizard of Oz*.

exploded. She was badly wounded and spent months in the hospital."[3]

```
                    INTER-OFFICE COMMUNICATION
        To   W K CRAIG-cc F L Hendrickson, K Weeks, MLeRoy
        Subject   MARGARET HAMILTON
        From  FRED DATIG        Date   1-5-39
```

          The above suffered first
degree burns on her face and second degree burns
on her hand in a scene which was being photographed
by us for our production WIZARD OF OZ on December
2 8th.

          Mr. Katz has advised that
Miss Hamilton is not to be taken off salary during
the period she is incapacitated.

          It is estimated she will
be able to resume her work in a week or ten days.

Memo noting Margaret getting burned during Oz filming on 12/28/1938

Margaret was referring to her stunt double, Betty Danko, who suffered permanent scars on one of her legs and required a hysterectomy because of the impact of the powerful blast.

Following the earlier accident of being burned in the Munchkinland scene, Margaret faced the unpleasant

---

[3] Betty was in the hospital for a couple of weeks, not months, per several accounts.

reality of having to deal with fire again, filming the movie's climactic scene in the witch's castle.

"I remember being very concerned that I had to grab a torch and set fire to Ray (Bolger – the Scarecrow). After an earlier experience when my broom caught fire, it was almost too much for me, but I was assured Bolger's suit was asbestos and there was little danger of its catching fire. Dorothy would then throw a bucket of water at Bolger that would, by chance, land on me, and I would begin to melt. This was to be the end of the witch."

Wicked Witch of the West's classic "I'm melting!" scene

Margaret's frightening cackle, a notable trait of the Wicked Witch of the West, became a recurring request over the years. When asked if she received coaching or training for her trademark cackle, she confidently told Howard Thompson in 1970, "The cackle was mine!"

Margaret Hamilton on Playing the Wicked Witch of the West

"The part was very fortunate for me. It's not often that a character actress gets a part that sticks in anyone's memory. I'm very grateful that it happened."

Cleveland Press (September 25, 1965)

"It's not the part I'd most like to be known for, but I don't mind."

The New York Times (March 14, 1970)

"I don't look on it as any great shakes of acting."

Newsday (March 19, 1978)

"I never had any idea of playing another witch (since having played a witch in a local theater production of *Macbeth* years before Oz), although I had loved *The Wizard of Oz* as a little girl and had talked about it while teaching kindergarten."

The Plain Dealer (October 13, 1978)

Margaret Hamilton on the Wicked Witch of the West's Effect on Youngsters

"It seemed to frighten children much more than I wished it had."

The New York Times (March 27, 1960)

"It's one of the ironies of my life. I don't think there is anyone who loves children more than I do, and now I'm famous for being the woman who scares children half to death."

The Plain Dealer (April 29, 1973)

On not reprising her Wicked Witch of the West role through the years despite many offers: "Little children's minds can't cope with seeing a mean witch alive again."

Yankee Magazine (October 1983)

Initial Reviews of Margaret Hamilton as the Wicked Witch of the West

"Miss Hamilton's grotesque witch is neatly drawn to gain dramatic effect."

Hollywood Reporter

"Margaret Hamilton triumphs as the Bad Witch."

Los Angeles Times

"Margaret Hamilton is magnificently evil as the dreadful witch."

Variety

Ironically, Margaret received a bland review from her hometown *Plain Dealer* newspaper:

"I really thought Margaret Hamilton's witch very real in make-up, but quite unreal in action and line of delivery."

The Plain Dealer movie critic W. Ward Marsh

Margaret's Relationship with Fellow Actors in *The Wizard of Oz*

Talking with Aljean Harmetz, author of *The Making of the Wizard of Oz*, Margaret noted, "Most people think that when the studios made movies, the key actors worked together a great deal of the time. But most of my scenes were with Judy (Garland) or the monkeys or just myself, and except for the early morning encounters in makeup, I saw almost nothing of the Lion, the Tin Woodman, or Ray Bolger, who, as the Scarecrow, had two scenes with me."

Margaret filmed more scenes with Judy Garland than the other cast members, allowing them to get to know each other. Stories written about the filming of *The Wizard of Oz* state Margaret was Judy's only adult friend on the set (she was only 16 during Oz). She shared in a 1970 New York Times interview, "Yes, I felt I knew Judy in a way, from two long talks on the set."

In a separate but related 1972 interview about her connection with Judy Garland on the set of Oz, Margaret recalled, "She was about to graduate from Hollywood High, and I helped her pick the dress, but she had to do a cross-promotional Oz tour and only got back the day before her last day at high school."

7
WITCHY WOMAN

Despite being one of the most successful films of 1939, *The Wizard of Oz* didn't achieve its current popularity until 1956, when it aired on network television for the first time. The movie became an annual family viewing tradition from 1959 to 1991. Starting in 1992, the film was seen more often with the advent of cable television.

The annual showing of *The Wizard of Oz* became a family television event, and the film's viewership grew immensely. Oz's unforgettable characters – Dorothy, the Tin Man, Scarecrow, Cowardly Lion, and the Wicked Witch of the West – became worldwide icons. Margaret Hamilton's Wicked Witch became the most frightening character ever known to generations of young children.

Margaret Hamilton received many requests to reprise her infamous role as the Wicked Witch of the West because of her character's fame. She politely declined all but a few offers to appear again as the Wicked Witch of the West, stating that "Little children's minds can't cope with seeing a mean witch alive again."

1959 marked the start of Oz's annual television presentation and its tremendous surge in popularity

Margaret Hamilton came somewhat close to recreating her Wicked Witch of the West character in a couple of movies. In the 1951 Bud Abbott and Lou Costello comedy *Comin' Round the Mountain,* she portrayed Aunt Huddy, a witch-like gypsy character who people sought after to provide a love potion. Sporting nearly identical nose and chin makeup, along with doing her famous witch-like cackle, Margaret almost was the Wicked Witch of the West.

Margaret Hamilton, as Aunt Huddy confronts the terrified duo of Abbott and Costello in *Comin' Round the Mountain*

One of the more popular movies Margaret appeared in was *13 Ghosts*, a horror film directed by William Castle. This film provided Castle an opportunity to pay homage to her Wicked Witch of the West character.

As *13 Ghosts* concludes, the inquisitive youngster Buck asks Margaret (as housekeeper Elaine), "You really are a witch, aren't you?" Hamilton replies sternly, "Ask me no questions, and I'll tell you no lies." After answering

Buck's question, Margaret's character, Elaine grabs a broom and makes a playful glance at the camera.

Margaret Hamilton in *13 Ghosts*

Another film director who paid homage to Margaret Hamilton and her Wicked Witch of the West persona was Robert Altman of *M*A*S*H movie fame. In *Brewster McCloud*, Margaret Hamilton's mean-spirited character Daphne Heap meets an untimely demise in the film; Altman provides moviegoers with a quick shot of Hamilton lying there in her long-coveted ruby slippers.

Margaret Hamilton finally gets her ruby slippers in *Brewster McCloud*, a little too late

Besides Margaret's movie-based witch roles, she reprised her Wicked Witch of the West persona several times on television.

Staying true to her roots as a children's advocate, Margaret made a special Wicked Witch of the West guest appearance on *Mister Rogers' Neighborhood*, where she helped defuse some fears associated with her scary *Wizard of Oz* character.

Margaret Hamilton and Fred Rogers

David Newell, then associate producer of *Mr. Rogers' Neighborhood*, pleaded to Hamilton in a brief letter to become one of the children's show's many guests. Newell recalled, "She wrote back and said, 'I'd be delighted to.'"

Margaret appeared on the May 14, 1975, show as the Wicked Witch of the West and gradually removed her makeup. She tried to assure the children watching that her witch character was just "make-believe" to reduce their fear and anxiety. Later in the episode, Mr. Rogers explained witches are just pretend and discussed the difference between real and make-believe things.

Campy comedic genius Paul Lynde's 1976 Halloween Special was truly a milestone in television history. The show featured a gracious Margaret Hamilton in a reprisal of the Wicked Witch of the West, introducing the members of the rock band KISS, who were making their network TV debut, to Paul Lynde and the audience. The special also featured Florence Henderson of *Brady Bunch* fame in various kinky outfits, Betty White, Billie Hayes (Witchiepoo from *H.R. PufnStuf*), and Donny and Maria Osmond as musical guests.

Margaret's visit to *Sesame Street* on the show's February 10, 1976, episode was clearly her most bizarre reprisal of her Wicked Witch of the West role.

In a Kenosha News interview before the show aired, Margaret noted, "I see no reason learning shouldn't be fun, and *Sesame Street* demonstrates that it can be a very happy experience." But Margaret's appearance on *Sesame Street* was not quite a happy experience for many of the show's young viewers. The episode drew complaints from many concerned parents after seeing the show's impact on their terrified children, leading to the controversial *Sesame Street* episode 847 being pulled from syndication.

```
                    MEMORANDUM
                Children's Television Workshop
                                        DATE  April 4, 1976

TO:     Sesame Street Producers, Writers, Joyce Acey

CC:

FROM:   Ana Herrera, Sesame Street Research

SUBJECT: MARGARET HAMILTON - THE WICKED WITCH OF THE WEST

        This memo is to report the results obtained from testing the segments
    of show 847, with Margaret Hamilton. Testing took place during March 1 to
    March 5 at Grant Day Care Center. A total of 26 children were observed,
    including 14 who were tested for comprehension. The show was viewed in
    color by 10 children and in B/W by 16 children. The objective of the study
    was to assess children's reactions to the Wicked Witch of the West. We
    were particularly interested in knowing if these segments were unusually
    fear arousing.

RECOMMENDATION:
Due to the parents' reactions, the contents of their letters, and our
impressions from group observation data, we suggest that the Margaret
Hamilton show not be re-run.
```

Excerpt from memo to pull the *Sesame Street*
episode featuring Margaret Hamilton from syndication

The premise of the episode featured the Wicked Witch of the West trying to retrieve her broom (that landed in *Sesame Street*) after losing it during a blustery flight across the sky. The witch's coercive tactics included threatening to "turn Big Bird into a feather duster" and making it rain in Mr. Hooper's store. It seemed the lesson to be learned on *Sesame Street* that day was how to deal with fear.

The only person on *Sesame Street* who enjoyed seeing the Wicked Witch of the West was the normally dour Oscar the Grouch. Upon meeting the witch, Oscar exclaims, "You know something? You have got to be the most beautiful person I have ever seen! Well, I think I'm in love!"

At the end of the episode, Margaret, as the Wicked Witch of the West, retrieves her broom in disguise (she appears as herself), quickly transforms back to the witch, lets out her trademark witch's cackle, and exclaims she's going to "Fly back to Oz as fast as lightning and never see *Sesame Street* again!"

Margaret Hamilton with Oscar the Grouch on *Sesame Street*

Perhaps her most obscure television show reprisal in a witch role was Margaret's appearance in *the Discovery '64* episode "The Weird World of Witchcraft." The ABC television show from October 25, 1964, discussed the history of sorcery and sorcerers from the Dark Ages to the witch hunts of Nazi Germany and included an interview with Margaret.

"The Weird World of Witchcraft" on *Discovery '64*

Airing right before Halloween on October 30, 1975, Margaret was the featured performer on the *CBS Radio Mystery* program "Triptych for a Witch." In the show, Margaret's villainous witch character masquerades as an elderly widowed distant relative, who moves in with a young newlywed couple. She is secretly a witch, joined by her strange pets – a talking cat and a parrot.

Besides reprising her Wicked Witch of the West role in movies and on television, Margaret appeared as the witch in several stage productions of *The Wizard of Oz* over the years. Margaret performed multiple times at St. Louis' Muny Theatre, besides acting at productions at Kansas City's Starlight Theatre and Casa Manana in Fort Worth.

Margaret Hamilton in the 1962
St. Louis Muny presentation of *The Wizard of Oz*

In a review of the 1962 Oz stage production, the *St. Louis Post* noted, "Margaret Hamilton, a veteran of the movie, was the Wicked Witch of the West, as gruesome as you could ask."

Along with Margaret making numerous reprisals of her Wicked Witch of the West role over the years, in 1974, she helped market Mego Corporation's "The Wicked Witch" doll/action figure.

Here's the official Mego description:

The Wicked Witch (Item No. 51500/6): The sixth in the line of *Mego Wizard of Oz* figures, this item recreates the character of the Wicked Witch of the West (Margaret Hamilton) from the film. The Wicked Witch comes on a standard female Mego body (jointed knees and elbows) cast in green with "ape hands." Her outfit consists of a plain black dress, a pair of black shoes, and a pointed witch's hat cast in black rubber. Her only accessory is her faithful broom, which comprises two pieces: the handle (brown) and the head (green).

 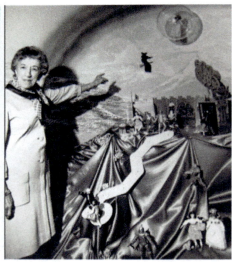

Margaret Hamilton at the 1975 New York Toy Fair posing with Mego Corporation's *The Wizard of Oz* line of dolls/action figures

The same year also saw Margaret's witch persona making a foray into pop culture by being featured on the popular Electric Light Orchestra (ELO) 1974 album cover "Eldorado."

There were various explanations for the use of *The Wizard of Oz's* image on "Eldorado's" album cover. Some believed that depicting the Wicked Witch of the West reaching for Dorothy's ruby slippers symbolized the unattainable, much like the search for El Dorado, the legendary city of gold.

A simpler explanation from Don Arden, the band's manager, was that the Oz imagery would be good for ELO's promotion, as it was quite recognizable to American audiences.

ELO "Eldorado" album cover

Pop art superstar Andy Warhol even immortalized Margaret's Wicked Witch of the West persona when he created his famous *Myths* portfolio of screen prints in 1981.

While attending a performance of the Peking Opera at New York's Metropolitan Opera House in August 1980 with Bianca Jagger, Andy spotted Margaret Hamilton in the crowd. As detailed in *The Andy Warhol Diaries*, "I saw

Margaret Hamilton, the witch in *The Wizard of Oz*, and got so excited and went over to her and told her how wonderful she was."

A year later, in 1981, Andy invited Margaret to be part of the *Myths* series. The prints were based upon imaginary iconic characters from Warhol's childhood, and he was delighted when Margaret accepted his offer to pose for one of his prints. Unlike many of his artworks based on images from mass-consumption media, Andy took several Polaroid photos from which to create his screen prints.

Andy Warhol photographing Margaret Hamilton

After taking many photographs of Margaret, Andy selected his favorite image of her. He titled the *Myths* screen print of Margaret Hamilton simply "The Witch."

Andy Warhol's favorite Polaroid he took of Margaret Hamilton

Putting his creative spin on the photo of Margaret, Andy created another classic pop-art classic of an American icon.

Afterward, Margaret was delighted to receive one of the finished prints as a gift from Andy.

"The Witch" from Andy Warhol's *Myths* series

Prominent doll artist Sheila Kwartler created a Margaret Hamilton-themed figurine for the United Federation of Doll Clubs 1982 convention. What made this doll unique is that it was created in collaboration with Margaret, capturing the likeness of her actual face. Each of the very rare 331 dolls also included a hand-signed label from Margaret attached to the cape.

"Margaret Hamilton" Portrait doll by artist Sheila Kwartler

8
MISS GULCH

Overshadowed by her iconic role as the Wicked Witch of the West, Margaret's equally evil performance as mean-spirited Almira Gulch was also a classic in its own right. Drawing upon her previous acting roles in which she played several rigid spinsters, Miss Gulch was a nasty composite of these characters.

After being bitten by Toto, Margaret, as Miss Gulch, delivered a cold-hearted demand to Dorothy and her Aunt Em and Uncle Henry, "That dog's a menace to the community. I'm taking him to the sheriff and make sure he's destroyed!" Few viewers can forget the ensuing scene and accompanying soundtrack as a stern-looking Miss Gulch propped up rigidly on her bicycle pedals furiously down the road with Toto stuffed inside her picnic basket.

Margaret Hamilton as Miss Gulch pedals angrily down the road

Margaret commented to Aljean Harmetz, "Miss Gulch was just like a hundred other parts I'd done. She was thin and she was skinny, and she was mean, and she was funny in her audacity and in her feeling of being just appalled at the simplest things. She was funny in her strictness and her hewing to the line and her insistence on certain things, regardless of whether she was right or wrong."

Harmetz sensed Margaret did not enjoy talking about Miss Gulch. Margaret stated, "When I watch her on television, I think she's too fast and too jerky. There's something about that characterization that I never really liked very well. Maybe I just don't like the lady. Maybe I don't like her taking that dog."

Upon meeting children who would recognize her as Miss Gulch, she would occasionally hear comments of "You were mean, you were really mean!" to which she'd typically reply, "I know, but I was just pretending." That was often followed up by comments from the children like, "When you took that dog, you were awful mean! I didn't like you at all – I don't like you yet."

Margaret would try her best to convince the children that she was acting, but often to no avail. She shared with the dinner crowd, "That's the thing I found that really sticks in their mind, and they have no use for that lady!"

Some interesting trivia about Miss Gulch in *The Wizard of Oz* is that in an early draft penned by writer Noel Langley, she had a son "Walter," and a Land of Oz counterpart named Bulbo, neither character making it into the final movie.

MISS GULCH RETURNS!

Margaret Hamilton's other role in *The Wizard of Oz*, as Miss Gulch, inspired musical director Fred Barton (*Forbidden Broadway*) to "accidentally" develop the satiric cabaret *Miss Gulch Returns!*

Barton's spectacle is billed as a "One-Man, One-Piano Metaphorical Musical Tour De Force."

When he was 11, Barton saw a touring production of *Oklahoma!* co-starring Hamilton and wrote to her as many enthralled children did over the years. Margaret responded to young Fred's captivating letter as she did with all the children who took the time to write to her.

At age 16, Barton sneaked backstage after a matinee in *A Little Night Music*, showing Hamilton the letter she had written to him five years earlier. Between scenes, Ms. Hamilton invited Barton to her dressing room, where she told him the secrets of melting and throwing fire.

In 1979, Barton filled a last-minute position as Miss Gulch for a *Wizard of Oz* summer revival. Doubling as music director, he played *Over the Rainbow* (in Gulch's costume) on an offstage piano and pedaled onstage; the crew could not stop laughing at the irony. Later, Barton expressed his emotions musically in a popular five-minute club routine on Miss Gulch.

Fred Barton as Miss Gulch

In 1983, Barton saw Margaret Hamilton for the last time, at the final *Wizard*-cast reunion; she was wise, philosophical, and funny, he recalls. "I was amazed. I thought: isn't it odd that the Wicked Witch turned out to be a wise, wonderful woman?"

Hamilton's resilience to attend the reunion, despite her health problems, inspired him. In November of that year, Barton released *Miss Gulch Lives!* – a collection of his songs and material borrowed from *The Wizard of Oz* – to use as a vehicle for himself. In 1985, he changed the title to *Miss Gulch Returns!* – hours before the *N.Y. Times* reported Hamilton's death.

Gulch is "much more than the sum of the parts," Barton notes. "It represents a complete photograph of my state of mind at the time."

"She's (Margaret Hamilton as Miss Gulch) a metaphor for me in a bad mood, for being self-defeatingly single. There are a million love songs, a million unrequited love songs. But when I wrote this, I felt there were not enough songs about people unable to fall in love, to begin with, or about people who can't even attract the attention of the person they want to love."

9

ITS FUNNY, BUT I FEEL AS IF I'VE KNOWN YOU ALL THE TIME

Margaret Hamilton's lengthy stage and film career found her crossing paths with her former Oz co-stars from time to time. Coincidentally, Margaret's next movie after Oz starred Judy Garland.

During the filming of *The Wizard of Oz*, Margaret developed the closest relationship of the cast members with Judy Garland. She always had a special place in her heart for Judy, which was ironic given the nature of her role as Dorothy's nemesis in Oz.

As *The Wizard of Oz* was wrapping up, the studio made a somewhat lame attempt to appease Margaret for getting seriously injured during filming.

She noted that "because I had been burned, as a sort of – I don't know exactly what kind of gesture it was, some sort of a thought to my injured feelings, I guess, only it wasn't the feelings that were hurt, I was asked to do a part in *Babes in Arms* with Judy and Mickey Rooney – a very tiny part."

1939's *Babes in Arms*

Margaret played mean-spirited Martha Steele in *Babes in Arms*, who once again harassed Judy's character in the film. Conservative busybody Martha Steele, as head of the town's welfare society, is against the local "vaudeville kids" who come from down-and-out families that can't support them. Miss Steele firmly states to the judge in the film, "My duty is concerned with those poor children. And something has got to be done about it." Her solution is that they are sent to the "state work school."

Instead of sending the show business kids away, the judge suggests a compromise: they must put on a show for the locals to prove their worthiness to stay in town. The somewhat ridiculous storyline of the movie allowed Judy Garland and Mickey Rooney to shine with their song and dance abilities.

Margaret recollected how, during the filming of *Babes in Arms*, Judy Garland was being mistreated by the film's director, Busby Berkeley, and that her overbearing mother did nothing about it. "Judy asked me to sit with her in her dressing room. That way, the mom couldn't have a temper tantrum. I smuggled her in cookies because she was kept on a starvation diet. I told Busby off once about his foul language (towards Judy)."

Margaret did not see Judy again until 1944. They would meet on the MGM movie set as Judy was wrapping up filming of her soon-to-be blockbuster *Meet Me in St. Louis*.

Margaret was shocked when she saw how thin Judy had become. "You're getting awfully thin, honey," Margaret told her. She replied, "I know, but I have to."

After hearing from the makeup woman how Judy had recently lost a lot of weight, Margaret wondered why she had to lose so much weight, thinking that it must not be good for her. When Margaret pressed the makeup woman for more information about Judy's condition, she was asked, "Well, do you think she seems the same Dorothy you knew?"

Following more conversation, Margaret learned Judy had become "difficult" and was having a tough time getting any rest. Judy was being given pills to rest and pills to wake up, all the while being pressured to keep her weight down and maintain a very busy schedule.

Margaret wouldn't see Judy again until 1951 at Broadway's Palace Theatre, where she was doing a series of concerts. Margaret visited Judy backstage with her close friend Donald Smith and was shocked when they met. Playwright John Ahlin, speaking years later with Donald, described how "a distraught Judy burst into tears upon seeing her old friend Margaret, grabbing her and exclaiming, 'Oh, my witch, my witch...' clinging to her like she was a child."

The next time Margaret would meet her friend again coincided with Judy's 1961 Carnegie Hall comeback performance. "I went backstage, and she didn't recognize me or Ray Bolger. He was in tears, saying she was on something," Margaret shared in a 1972 interview published in *Conversations with Classic Film Stars*.

In 1968, there was a happier reunion when Judy Garland was scheduled to appear as a guest on Merv Griffin's TV talk show in the fall. The show's producers thought it would be a great idea to have Margaret surprise Judy on the show. Judy and Margaret hadn't seen each other in years, and Margaret was worried that Judy wouldn't recognize her.

Margaret told them, "Well, I want you to know something. It might be a surprise, it might be an awful shock, and we haven't seen each other for years. I've changed, and she might very easily look at me and not be sure who I am, and then it wouldn't be very funny – I didn't want to do that to her, and I won't."

A month later, the producers from *The Merv Griffin Show* contacted Margaret again about coming on the show. This time, the producers detailed how Judy would substitute for Merv as guest host and emphasized that Judy had already approved the idea of Margaret appearing on the show. Margaret still had concerns and asked the producers again, "Are you sure you're telling me the truth?" After telling her they were, Margaret reiterated, "I want to be sure because I can tell you it may not be very funny if she doesn't know who I am."

Margaret finally appeared on *The Merv Griffin Show* episode that was filmed on December 19, 1968, which was seen in syndication by most viewers on January 2, 1969. To make it to the show, she had to skip out on the first day of practice for the new Broadway play *Come Summer*, starring Oz alum Ray Bolger. Arriving on the set of *The Merv Griffin Show*, the plan was to have Judy stroll down the aisle on the way to the stage and shake hands with all the people in the front row where Margaret would be sitting. When Judy came upon Margaret, she was to step back and exclaim, "Haven't I seen you before!!?" to which Margaret would do her best "Heh-heh-heh," Wicked

Witch cackle, and then Judy would turn and run up on stage.

Because of the overwhelming applause that greeted Judy when the show started (as she walked down the aisle) and never subsided until she got up on stage, the planned encounter with Margaret was drowned out by the ongoing applause and never happened.

During their brief segment together Judy exclaims, "You're my favorite witch!" to which Margaret enthusiastically replies riposted, "I'd better be!" Judy then adds, "I think you're everybody's favorite lady."

After plugging Margaret's upcoming play *Come Summer*, Judy wanted her to "Laugh! Just do that wicked, mean laugh!" After a little coaxing, Margaret did indeed do her famous witch cackle, much to the delight of Judy and the audience.

Years later, in an interview, Margaret recalled, "I did a *Merv Griffin Show* with her, and her speech was slurred. I realized the sweet little teenager I'd known was long gone."

Margaret and Judy on *The Merv Griffin Show*

The 1950s represented the golden era of live television, providing Margaret with the opportunity to do plenty of work beyond her traditional maid and spinster movie roles. Live television also allowed Margaret to work several times with Oz costar Bert Lahr. As their two live 1950s television performances occurred before the annual televising of *The Wizard of Oz*, there was minimal fanfare in their reunion.

Margaret Hamilton and Bert Lahr television appearances together:

1953 U.S. Steel Hour - *You Can't Win*

1954 *Best of Broadway - The Man Who Came to Dinner*

1960 *The Secret World of Eddie Hodges*

Bert Lahr, who played the Cowardly Lion

Margaret also collaborated with Jack Haley, the Tin Man, in 1945's highly acclaimed comedy *George White's*

Scandals. In the movie, Jack and Margaret played siblings, with George White (Haley) unable to wed until his sister Annabelle is betrothed.

The comedy plays out as a no-nonsense Annabelle has no qualms about preventing her brother's pending engagement. Margaret's character delivers a couple of classic lines towards her brother's fiancée. After the fiancé asks why she doesn't like her, Annabelle's swift response is, "You're an utter monstrosity!" Later in the film, after being tricked by the fiancée, an angry Annabelle exclaims, "I'll pull your blonde hair out by its black roots!" and flings an axe at her.

Jack Haley, Joan Davis, and Margaret in *George White's Scandals*

Margaret made several appearances years later with Haley at Oz-related events but had minimal contact with him off-camera in both of their movies together.

The Daydreamer (1966) was the only other movie in which Oz costars Margaret Hamilton and Ray Bolger appeared together, apart from *The Wizard of Oz*. The movie was a lighthearted drama about children's author Hans Christian Andersen and featured actors interspersed with Rankin and Bass (of *Rudolph the Red-Nosed Reindeer* fame) animated characters.

Bolger had the opportunity to showcase his magnificent dancing skills as "The Pieman" in the movie, while Margaret was given the role of the crabby Mrs. Klopplebobbler.

Movie poster for *The Daydreamer*

The Broadway musical *Come Summer* offered Margaret Hamilton another chance to work with Ray Bolger after their film roles in 1966's *The Daydreamer*. Panned by critics, the production was short-lived and left Bolger with bitterness towards the theater critics who reviewed the play.

Lasting only seven performances, *Come Summer* lost a significant amount of money. One positive was that Margaret received a couple of good theatrical reviews while performing her role of Dorinda Pratt, a hard-nosed New England matron.

Poster from *Come Summer* featuring Ray Bolger and Margaret Hamilton

As *The Wizard of Oz* became a beloved annual family TV tradition, there was a surge in Oz-themed specials and festivals, leading to several cast reunions.

Margaret took part in many Oz-themed events, always taking great care in trying to either confirm or dispel stories associated with the making of the film. A myth she tried to dispel several times were stories of how the actors portraying the munchkins were a bunch of drunks – a contention Margaret always denied.

Margaret Hamilton reunites in 1970 with
Oz compatriots Ray Bolger and Jack Haley

Over the years, people have often wondered if the famous witches of Oz were friends or appeared in any other film, television, or theater productions together.

They appeared in an obscure March 18, 1951, episode on *The Bigelow Theatre* entitled "Dear Amanda" on television. Surprisingly, there was no media fanfare of any kind regarding their reunion.

In her 1949 memoir *With a Feather on My Nose*, Billie Burke barely discusses *The Wizard of Oz* – with no mention of Margaret Hamilton at all. The 2009 book *Mrs. Ziegfeld: The Public and Private Lives of Billie Burke,* once again, omits Billie having any kind of relationship with her fellow Oz cast members, including Margaret.

Similarly, in several interviews over the years, Margaret made very few comments about Billie. Margaret mentioned her subpar dressing room while filming Oz compared to the elegant one Billie had as a more established star.

Billie Burke as Glinda

The animated *Journey Back to Oz*, released in 1974, featured an all-star cast and provided Margaret Hamilton with the opportunity to supply the voice of Auntie Em versus her classic Wicked Witch of the West character. The movie also featured Judy Garland's daughter, Liza Minelli, who portrayed the voice of Dorothy in the film.

Journey Back to Oz featured the voices of
Margaret Hamilton and Judy Garland's daughter, Liza Minnelli

Judy Garland's other daughter, Lorna Luft, played Almira Gulch/the Wicked Witch of the West in a Manchester (England) production of *The Wizard of Oz* in December 2008. In an interview, Lorna said, "I've always tried to stay away from that one piece of history in my family because it's so iconic. But when they offered me the role of the Wicked Witch, to be honest with you, they made me an offer I couldn't refuse!"

Judy Garland's youngest daughter,
Lorna Luft, as the Wicked Witch of the West

Margaret Hamilton and Toto (actually Terry, a Cairn terrier) appeared together in three movies. In addition to *The Wizard of Oz*, Margaret and Terry were together in 1938's *Stablemates*, the film they made just before *The Wizard of Oz*. They were reunited one last time in the 1942 film *Twin Beds*, which featured Margaret in one of her many movie maid roles.

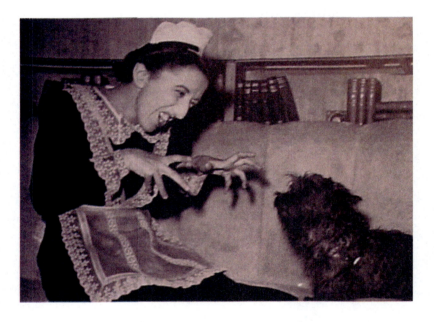

Margaret Hamilton gets reacquainted with Toto (Terry) in a *Twin Beds* publicity photo

Margaret spoke kindly about Toto (Terry), describing how, during the filming of *Oz*, he "was a darling little dog. I think he was almost worked to death."

10
AFTER OZ

Margaret's movie career in the years following *The Wizard of Oz* continued to see her primarily portray characters as the town gossip, feisty spinster, or her most frequent role as a maid. In most of these roles, Margaret's appearance in the movie was brief, with minimal dialogue. She maximized these limited roles with a polished technique of delivering her lines in a snappy, feisty tone, coupled with an expressive glance or nod, often stealing the scene.

Margaret preferred the stage over her movie roles but realized the practicality of getting steady work as a character actress. The uncertainty that comes with working in a theatrical production that could be canceled with short notice was a situation she wanted to avoid. Having a steady paycheck was important in her capacity as a single mother raising her young son.

"I've done some hard-bitten parts, but most of the time, I'm the cantankerous cook or the acidulous aunt with a corset of steel and a heart of gold," she once exclaimed.

Margaret Hamilton in *These Three,*
one of the many times she played a maid

Margaret never expressed discontent with these confined roles and remained thankful for the consistent work, unlike her peers, who frequently struggled to find their next acting opportunity.

She continued to live in California after the filming of Oz, churning out a steady stream of movies as a character actress, several of which are featured on the following pages.

My Little Chickadee

On a few rare occasions, Margaret got the opportunity to go beyond playing her customary movie roles with their corresponding limited dialogue. In the movie *My Little Chickadee*, she had an expanded role in which she got to highlight her comedic skills.

1940's *My Little Chickadee* was the only movie in which screen legends W. C. Fields and Mae West appeared together. Mae wrote most of the screenplay and was primarily responsible for casting her fellow actors in the film.

Margaret commented in a 1968 interview with Richard Lamparski how grateful she was to have been selected by Mae to appear in the movie as town gossip Mrs. Gideon. In the film, Mrs. Gideon repeatedly warns everyone about the moral shortcomings of Mae West's Flower Belle Lee character. A prudish Mrs. Gideon tells Cuthbert J. Twillie (W. C. Fields) that there is nothing good about Flower Belle. In classic W. C. Fields fashion, Twillie deadpans, "I can see what's good. Tell me the rest."

Margaret noted candidly that Mae had somewhat of an inflated opinion about herself and said to her, "Can I help it if every man on this set is crazy in love with me?" To which Margaret jokingly remarked in her Lamparski interview, "Well, the love was one-sided, I can tell you. She was forty-eight and needed special lighting to wash out her creases."

As for the top-hatted braggadocios W.C. Fields, Margaret had nothing but praise and kind words. Upon meeting him, Margaret comments, "Bill Fields walked in the first day, reeking of liquor. He came over and apologized to me. Understand, I was in awe of his talents. I said, 'Mr. Fields, on you, it smells like cologne,' and he brightened up."

Margaret further adds about W.C. Fields, "I just adored that man. He was the most wonderful person. I think I never laughed more than I did making that picture, before or since. He was the finest gentleman on the set." Margaret observed that despite his gruff appearance, W. C. Fields didn't use obscene language and was nothing like the character he played other than perhaps enjoying his liquor.

Cuthbert J. Twillie (W. C. Fields), Flower Belle Lee (Mae West) and Margaret Hamilton (Mrs. Gideon) in *My Little Chickadee*

Johnny Come Lately

Margaret got the chance to work with another screen legend, James Cagney, in 1943's *Johnny Come Lately*. In the movie, Margaret played another of her standard busybody roles. Reflecting on her work with James Cagney, she stated that he "was a painstaking actor, rehearsed in great detail, and was always interesting to watch and work with."

Cagney and Hamilton later both lived in the same 34 Gramercy Park East apartment building in New York City. A historical marker by the apartment building commemorates their residency.

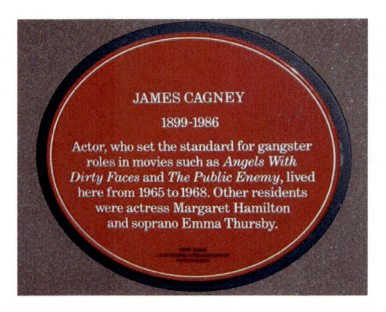

James Cagney in *Johnny Come Lately* speaks as Margaret Hamilton looks on suspiciously

State of the Union

In *State of the Union* (1948), Margaret Hamilton played the role of housemaid Norah, which featured the legendary Katharine Hepburn and Spencer Tracy.

Commenting on working with Katharine Hepburn, Margaret praised her as being "very straightforward and direct and one of the nicest, kindest, and most generous people I have ever worked with… I just loved her."

Margaret Hamilton with Katharine Hepburn in *State of the Union*

Elaborating with close friend Wesley Wehr on her fondness for Katherine, she said, "I had only a small part, but Miss Hepburn was so kind to me. The director wasn't satisfied with the way I spoke my few lines. He was impatient. He wanted to move along to the next scene. Miss Hepburn stopped him and told him firmly: 'This is Margaret's best moment in the film. We're not going to go on until it's just right.' Can you imagine a star as famous as Katherine Hepburn being that thoughtful toward a minor performer such as me?"

The Invisible Woman

The Invisible Woman (1940) starred the legendary John Barrymore as a bumbling professor who discovers the key to invisibility. Margaret Hamilton was in the movie as Mrs. Jackson, the professor's faithful housekeeper. The filmmakers modeled the film after the popular 1933 movie, *The Invisible Man*.

Weekend television horror hosts often showcase *The Invisible Woman*, discussing its associated trivia:

- Legendary actor John Barrymore being the grandfather of Drew Barrymore
- Shemp Howard of *Three Stooges* fame playing a gangster in the film
- Margaret appears more often in the movie than the star, Virgina Bruce (because she's invisible!)

Jonn Barrymore and Margaret Hamilton in *The Invisible Woman*

Shemp Howard   Drew Barrymore

Margaret would appear in over 70 films throughout her lengthy career. She worked with several famed directors, including Victor Fleming, Frank Capra, Busby Berkeley, Joseph L. Mankiewicz, Fritz Lang, Michael Curtiz, William A. Wellman, Robert Altman, and horror master William Castle.

Besides the actors already noted, Margaret had the pleasure of working in movies featuring Golden Age of Hollywood comedy superstars Buster Keaton, Oliver Hardy (minus Stan Laurel), Harold Lloyd, and Irene Ryan - better known later as Granny on *The Beverly Hillbillies*. She was also in early movies with Cary Grant in *People Will Talk*, a very young Natalie Wood in *Driftwood*, and Bing Crosby in *Riding High* - a remake of her earlier film *Broadway Bill*.

But even though she was in many movies with high-profile stars, it didn't necessarily mean Margaret would get the chance to get to talk with them, let alone get to know them. Margaret noted in several interviews that she often had minimal interaction with other actors in the movie unless they were in the same scene. Margaret shared an amusing story about how she invited friend and fellow actress Sara Haden to attend a recent movie she had a part in. While watching the movie together, they realized they were both in the movie – without ever seeing each other on the set, resulting in a few laughs.

Despite Margaret's ongoing movie career and the financial stability that filmmaking brought, her first love of appearing on stage remained. She noted, "If it wasn't for the financial advantages and the certainty of constant work, I would never consider films for a moment. The mechanics count for so much in pictures. You feel that only about one-tenth of the picture is you and nine-tenths something or somebody else. Often, they cut the very scene that you love the best. And then you can't go out and get your own job in a picture; you have to have an agent and take what is handed to you. I still prefer free-lancing to contracts in films."

After a couple of years of playing character actress roles in movies, Margaret's desire to be on stage again led to her doing summer stock in 1941. She appeared in many plays at the Lakewood Theatre in Madison, Maine, which describes itself today as "the State Theater of Maine and *America's oldest and most famous summer theater.*"

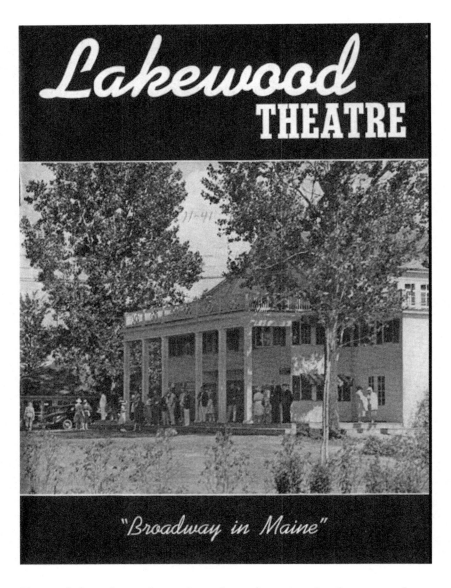

Two of the plays she enjoyed performing in the most that summer at the Lakewood Theatre were *Skylark* and *Ladies in Retirement*.

Lakewood Players in "Skylark"

Here are the Lakewood Players after a rehearsal of "Skylark", the current comedy. Front row, left to right, Elaine Perry, Byron McGrath, Margaret Hamilton and Gene Knudsen. Standing at left, Jack Tyler. Center row, left to right, Russell Hardie, Ann Mason, Joseph Sweeney. Standing at right, Melville Burke, stage director. Back row, from left, Bob Hays, assistant and Elmer Hall, stage manager; Grant Mills and Allan Tower.

Margaret Hamilton (bottom row) with the Lakewood Players

Margaret expressed her joy at being able to perform again at Lakewood Theatre: "I was glad to get back on stage. I wondered if I would still be able to learn parts. One of the oddest things was my reaction to laughs. I'd been so long without them that they sounded strange. I'd almost forgotten about the building, the feeding and killing of them. But it all came back."

Margaret Hamilton who comes to Lakewood this season after six years in Hollywood where she has appeared in such films as "The Invisible Woman," "The Wizard of Oz," "The Farmer Takes A Wife," and "The Moon's Our Home," will have the Flora Robson role in next week's thrilling melodrama "Ladies in Retirement."

One story written about Margaret's summer stock performances at Lakewood Theatre focused on her young son Hamilton (then nicknamed "Tony"). A local Maine newspaper interviewed both Margaret and her then 5-year-old son Tony, as he whimsically critiqued her performances in a couple of plays – sometimes not that flattering of a review either. He seemed to enjoy, like any young child, those plays and roles that were more fun and humorous than anything more serious and boring.

Margaret noted this was the first time her son had been to see a play and had not yet seen a movie either, including *The Wizard of Oz*. She detailed how the closest Tony came to seeing his mother in a movie was through discovering some movie stills of her as the Wicked Witch of the West by accident at home. He couldn't believe it was her until she admitted it. Later, he would show visitors to their home pictures of "My mother, the witch."

The same article also mentions how they fell in love with Maine, enjoying a summer of boat rides, horseback riding, and canoeing. The Maine woods, lakes, and brooks were nothing like he had ever experienced back home in Beverly Hills.

The Maine adventures Tony experienced were of utmost importance to Margaret as part of her strategy to raise her young son as a normal child. Margaret noted how, while filming Oz, MGM studio head Louis B. Mayer wanted to offer her good-looking son "a kiddie contract. 'Don't you dare!' I shouted, and he ran off. I'd seen, upfront, the awful things Hollywood did to little children."

Excerpt of the story featuring Margaret's young son, Hamilton "Tony" Meserve

Margaret and her son grew fond of Maine that summer while she was performing on stage at the Lakewood Theatre. Years later, when looking in Maine with her son and daughter-in-law to purchase a summer cottage, they came upon the unexpected fact that Cape Island, located off the tip of the village of Cape Newagen, was for sale. They promptly purchased the 20-acre island, complete with an 1852 farmhouse, and Margaret began staying there by herself for the summer from 1961 through the early 1980s.

Margaret was often spotted rowing between the mainland and the island. Her island schedule fluctuated because of work, and she frequently hosted friends. She came to know many of the mainland residents across the water, who became enchanted to know her.

Some tour boat operators and locals affectionately named her place "Witch Island."

Cape Island, Maine, aka "Witch Island"
– Margaret's "summer cottage" below

For Margaret and young Tony, life back in Beverly Hills was both busy and enjoyable. After her divorce in 1938, they would spend over a decade living at a couple of residences in Beverly Hills on North Canon Drive and later on North Elm Drive. Margaret adeptly handled the demanding task of raising her son alone while also pursuing a career in acting, which was particularly uncommon back then.

When Margaret and Tony were living on North Canon Drive in Beverly Hills, one of their nearby neighbors was famed comedian Harpo Marx, his wife Susan, and their four children. The two families became very close.

Bill Marx, the oldest of the Marx children, was closest in age to young Tony, and they both attended Hawthorne School while living there. In his autobiography, Bill Marx comments, "Margaret Hamilton was one of the wonderfully special people to grace our planet, despite us all knowing her as the dreaded Wicked Witch of the West in *The Wizard of Oz*. She was as good in real life as she was evil in that movie."

Bill mentioned how his mother Susan and Margaret were both members of the PTA and "just like my mom, Maggie managed to schedule tenure as a Cub Scout den mother when nobody else wanted to be one."

Margaret was recruited by existing members to run for the Beverly Hills Unified School District Board of Education. She ran, won, and served on the governing board from 1948 to 1951 under her married name, Meserve.

Neighbor Harpo Marx of the famed Marx Brothers

[216]

In addition to Bill Marx saying kind things about Margaret, he had this to say about Tony, "the only thing I ever disliked about him was that he was so much smarter than everybody else. Strait-laced, forthright, and dripping with Ivy League, you couldn't help but figure then that he would be odds-on-favorite to become a model citizen, which of course he became."

When Bill thinks of Tony, "a sad and heartwarming event in his life comes to mind." The event Bill is referring to was the first time Tony saw *The Wizard of Oz* at a classmate's birthday party. Michael Berman's birthday party included a special screening of Oz in their home theater for Tony and the other kids. During the Oz viewing, Tony ran out of the room when he saw his mom dressed as the Wicked Witch of the West.[4]

Returning home after the party, Tony wondered what had happened to the witch's Winkie guards after she melted. Margaret had to explain to Tony multiple times

---

[4] Multiple/slightly different versions describing the first time Tony saw *The Wizard of Oz* are told by: 1) Margaret Hamilton in the book *The Making of The Wizard of Oz*, 2) Bill Marx in his autobiography *Son of Harpo Speaks!* and 3) several magazine and newspaper interviews with Ham (Tony) Meserve over the years.

that everything in the film was fictional but finally reassured him that the guards were free after the witch melted and simply wanted to return home.

As Bill Marx predicted early on, Hamilton (Tony) Meserve went on to have a very productive business career in international banking, publishing, and even running an antique store with his wife, Helen. They were proud parents of three children and Margaret often spoke glowingly of them in many interviews she did over the years.

Margaret shared how, because her son Ham was working overseas, she'd usually go abroad annually to visit her grandkids. She took trips to Korea, India, and even Saudi Arabia to see her family.

Retired from banking, Ham is a longtime County Commissioner in Lincoln County, Maine, was board president of the nearby Harbor Theater, and has been part of many community organizations, following his mother's passion for public service.

Hamilton Meserve

Living next door to Margaret on North Canon Drive in Beverly Hills was actor Ralph Bellamy, best known to movie audiences as one of the millionaire brothers in the comedy *Trading Places*. Bellamy, like Margaret, had a firm commitment to service and advocacy, which he used to bring about many positive changes to actors in the theatrical field. He served as Vice President of the Actors Equity Association and later was the organization's President for three straight terms, fighting for improved working conditions and better pay.

Margaret, following her neighbor's example, served on the Actors Equity Association Council.

Ralph Bellamy with Don Ameche
and Eddie Murphy in *Trading Places*

Continuing to play small character actress roles in the movies, Margaret looked forward to returning to the stage one day again after performing in the Lakewood

Theatre summer stock productions. After nearly a decade of absence from Broadway, Margaret found a wonderful opportunity to return there in late 1943.

Margaret was thrilled to be reunited with several friends of hers when performing on Broadway in *Outrageous Fortune* at the Forty-Eighth Street Theatre. The play was both written and staged by Rose Franken, the playwright of *Hallam Wives/Another Language*, in which Margaret had her breakthrough Broadway role and later movie version. Also in the cast of *Outrageous Fortune* was Maria Ouspenkaya, her former drama teacher and renowned actress.

FORTY-EIGHTH STREET
THEATRE

EMERGENCY NOTICE: In the event of an alert, remain in your seats. A competent staff has been trained for this emergency. Keep calm. You will receive information and instructions from the stage.   F. H. La GUARDIA, Mayor

FIRE NOTICE: The exit indicated by a red light and sign nearest to the seat you occupy is the shortest route to the street. In the event of fire please do not run—WALK TO THAT EXIT.
Patrick Walsh, Fire Commissioner and Chief of Department

It is urged for the comfort and safety of all, that theatre patrons refrain from lighting matches in this theatre.

THE · PLAYBILL · A · WEEKLY · PUBLICATION · OF · PLAYBILL · INCORPORATED

Week beginning Sunday, November 21, 1943   •   Matinees Wednesday and Saturday

WILLIAM BROWN MELONEY
presents

ELSIE FERGUSON
in

OUTRAGEOUS FORTUNE
by
ROSE FRANKEN
with

| MARIA OUSPENSKAYA | MARGALO GILLMORE |
| FREDERIC TOZERE | MARGARET HAMILTON |

As usual, Margaret received a favorable theatrical review in *Outrageous Fortune* for her portrayal of Gertrude Goldsmith, the doctor's wife in the play, who "injects just the right note of comedy into the proceedings."

The next time Margaret would appear on Broadway while residing in Beverly Hills was in 1948's *The Men We Marry*. Unfortunately, the play was a major flop and only lasted three days on Broadway. Reviews of the play were scathing, with the *New York Times* stating: "The only thing remarkable about *The Men We Marry* is that anyone should have thought that it was good enough to put on the stage."

Though Margaret's return to Broadway after a four-year absence was a bit of a disappointment for her, it allowed her to perform with distant relative Neil Hamilton, best known later on to television viewers as Commissioner Gordon on the 1960s hit show, *Batman*.

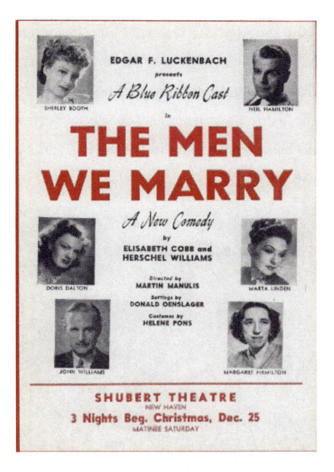

Over the ensuing decades, Margaret would periodically appear on Broadway again, along with several touring stage productions, never veering far from the joy that performing on stage brought her.

While still living in Beverly Hills, Margaret harkened back to her early days as a kindergarten and nursery school teacher and opened a preschool in the community.

In 1950, she founded the Beverly Hills Presbyterian Preschool at the corner of Rodeo Drive and Santa Monica Boulevard. She taught at the preschool as Mrs. Meserve, once again using her surname. The school remains open today and has been a fixture in the Beverly Hills community for decades.

Beverly Hills Presbyterian Preschool circa 1950

One of Margaret's young students was Lorraine Brodek, who reminisced that her "fondest memory at the church was when I was a seven-year-old student there. My teacher was Margaret Mesereve. The kids loved her because she had the best sense of humor – not what one would expect when you're supposed to be focusing on Jesus and memorizing your prayers."

Lorraine recalled how, one Sunday, Mrs. Meserve was able to take the young children in her class to see a rerun of *The Wizard of Oz* at a nearby theater despite some reservations from a few parents. She coincidentally sat next to Mrs. Meserve, and after watching the initial terrifying appearance of The Wicked Witch of the West in Munchkinland, she started crying. Lorraine was shocked as Mrs. Meserve put her reassuring arm around her and stated, "'Lorraine, it's okay. Look… I'm the witch! Only they put green makeup on me for the movie. Don't be afraid.' None of us knew. Why didn't our parents tell us she was the green witch in *The Wizard of Oz*? Outside, she tossed her head back as she cackled, 'I'll get you my pretties and your little dog too!'" much to the delight of all the children.

The Hamiltons' stay in California ended when Ham graduated eighth grade from Hawthorne. They moved to the East Coast, with Margaret living in New York, to once again be near the theater, while Ham went to the prestigious St. George's boarding school in Newport, Rhode Island, where he starred in tennis. "It was brutal," said Ham. "Going into a private school of wealthy kids in the Eastern establishment, I was a kid from California. I still have the scars."

11
NEW YORK NEW YORK

In the early 1950s, Margaret returned to New York City, living on East 48th Street near the Broadway stage she so adored. This coincided with a major change in the entertainment industry. Following World War II's end, commercial television's rise grew exponentially. Before 1947, few Americans owned television sets. By 1955, half of American homes had a TV set, and television soon replaced radio as the most popular home entertainment medium.

Before the advent of television, Margaret appeared on many radio programs, including three appearances on the *Rudy Vallee Show*, a musical variety show. One of these appearances included a 1933 radio show featuring future *Oz* actor Bert Lahr.

A whole galaxy of stars will be figuratively waiting for you on your front doorstep if you get home by 5 o'clock tonight. Rudy Vallee, KGO, will present the following on his program: Margaret Hamilton of "In Another Language," Osgood Perkins in a scene from "Front Page," Bert Lahr, comedian; Helen Lynd, comedienne and Georgie Lyons, jazz harpist.

[227]

The Lux Radio Theatre presented Broadway plays, and in May 1937, Margaret reprised her role as Helen Hallam in the radio version of *Another Language*. This would be the fourth adaptation of Margaret playing Helen, adding to her growing resume performances of the role in summer stock, on Broadway, and in the 1933 movie.

Lux Radio Theatre in New York City

The shift of popularity in the 1950s from radio to television initially benefited Margaret. The early part of the decade featured most television shows being broadcast live from New York City and were based on theatrical themes. Margaret's stage experience made her a perfect fit for live television performances, where she continued to excel in various character actress roles on shows like *The Gulf Playhouse, Medallion Theatre, Campbell Summer Soundstage, Center Stage,* and *The Best of Broadway.*

In the late 1950s, several television genres emerged and continue to be popular today, such as police and medical dramas, soap operas, westerns, game/quiz shows, and situational comedies. Changes that came with the introduction of new television show genres negatively affected Margaret's career in the late 1950s. Television's shift away from its early live theatrical shows somewhat limited her future opportunities. The programming shift, along with the fact that most television programs were soon being produced in Hollywood, further limited her television prospects in New York City. And she didn't want to move back out west.

And thinking back to those days out west, Margaret contemplated what opportunities she had earlier that might be available in New York City. She acted in early product publicity films, including a 1946 promo for Westinghouse's electric cooking appliances. In the promo, Margaret is a contemptuous nurse who accompanies an uncle to his relative's dinner party, aptly named "Dinner at 6."

Margaret as a nurse in Westinghouse's "Dinner at 6" promo

Thus, Margaret wondered if the evolution of 1950s television might provide some new opportunities for her through television commercials. She was successful in landing a prior engagement as the voice of Emily Tipp in the animated Tip-Top Bread commercials, urging television viewers to go buy this fine bread so they might enjoy that "Tip Top feeling."

Emily Tipp (aka Margaret Hamilton) with her Tip-Top bread

Margaret also did some commercials as the stressed-out woman in the Jell-O pudding "busy day" commercials. In the commercials, Margaret's animated character urged viewers to save time by preparing quick and easy, delicious Jell-O to make their day a little easier to handle.

Margaret's "busy day" Jell-O lady deals with a screaming baby, a ringing phone, and a knock on the door as she tries in vain to do some housework

Later in the 1950s, Margaret appeared in several other television and print advertisements.

[231]

As Safety Plate (windshield) pitchwoman "Prudence," Margaret tried to convince her friend Abigail about the benefits of Safety Plate Glass. She explained how the product would keep Abigail's car cooler while providing better vision than regular glass, making her driving experience "not so tiring on your eyes."

Margaret also appeared in what can be described as an infomercial, highlighting Pullman Company's luxurious sleeper cars. Margaret playfully showed the features of the elegant train car while Arlene Francis, who was both the hostess and a real-life friend, provided the details.

Show host Arlene Francis narrates as
Margaret reviews the Pullman train car

Fast forwarding a bit, Margaret's second most popular role of her career was that of spokesperson Cora for Maxwell House coffee commercials in the 1970s. What most people don't realize is these Maxwell House commercials were the most lucrative income she received for any role in her acting career, including *The Wizard of Oz*.

Margaret Hamilton as Maxwell House spokeswoman Cora

A no-nonsense New England shopkeeper who sold only Maxwell House coffee, Cora became an immensely popular television character. She never missed an opportunity to brew up a feisty blend of advice along with her beloved Maxwell House.

A typical commercial featured Cora offering a customer a cup of coffee as they browsed in her general store. After a sip of coffee, they inevitably asked what kind of coffee they were enjoying; Cora quickly retorted, "I only sell one kind – Maxwell House!"

The commercial usually ended with Cora stating, "Like they say – good to the last drop!"

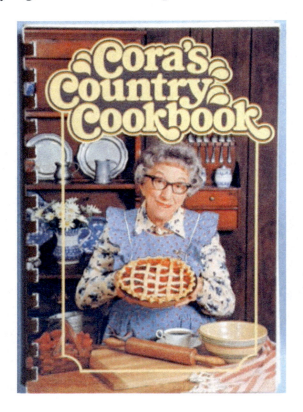

The popularity of Cora's character led to the creation of *Cora's Country Cookbook,* featuring down-home recipes

Margaret found auditioning for the role of Cora in the Maxwell House coffee commercials an arduous task. "It began when I went to a 'cattle call' audition attended by practically every character on Broadway," she said. "We read scripts but didn't know what it was all about, although it was obviously selling something."

The auditioning process, with its confidentiality and incessant revisions, was a confusing ordeal for Margaret. "I was called back again a week later to make a test of it, but they kept making changes and getting approval from the top echelons. A lawyer was on the set at all times to avoid fodder for a lawsuit," she said. "They gave me a retainer contract from March until August while the commercial was tested on TV. The tests went very well, and I got a firm contract."

The filming location for the Maxwell House coffee commercials was a century-old general store outside Stamford, Connecticut. Margaret noted, "An absolute mob of people sitting on a hillside across the way watch the commercials being made."

Two Maxwell House commercials with Cora featured future TV actors David Caruso (*NYPD Blue*) and Judd Hirsch (of *Taxi* fame) when they were very young.

The outstanding success of the Maxwell House coffee commercials earned enough royalties to establish a trust fund for Margaret's grandchildren. Close friend Wesley Wehr ironically noted in *The Eighth Lively Art*, he was dying of curiosity and "I checked Margaret's kitchen cabinets to see which kind of coffee she was using... She had freeze-dried Yuban coffee on her shelf!"

Margaret struggled somewhat through the mid-1950s, trying to land what was now a few character actress television roles available in New York City. She received an unexpected opportunity to be a regular cast member on the pioneering television comedy show *Ethel and Albert*. Margaret made a lifelong friend in the process - Peg Lynch, the show's writer and star, along with her young daughter Lisa.

The groundbreaking comedy *Ethel and Albert*, as well as its later radio version, *The Couple Next Door*, are both remarkable and historically significant for several reasons. Peg Lynch, who created the show, wrote every single episode by herself – over 10,000 scripts, *and* starred in both the radio and television versions. The show, in its various forms, went from the 1940s through the mid-1950s, along with even later radio incarnations in the 1960s and 1970s.

Ethel and Albert centered on the funny adventures of a middle-aged married couple famous for their light-hearted arguments. Peg reached out to Margaret to gauge her interest in playing the whimsical character of Aunt Eva on the show. "Margaret Hamilton and I hit it off immediately from the moment she walked on the set," Peg recalled.

Talking about performing on *Ethel and Albert* in a radio interview, Margaret shared, "I think it was about the nicest thing I ever did, and I loved every minute of it, and Peg was so wonderful; I think it was so great we were all so fond of each other."

Ethel (Peg Lynch), Albert (Alan Bunce), and Aunt Eva (Margaret Hamilton)

Margaret on the set of *Ethel and Albert*

They became so close that Peg's daughter soon came to know Margaret as "Aunt Maggie," and likewise, Lisa affectionately became known as "Pumpkin Pie." Margaret would even come over to Peg's house for Halloween a couple of times, dressing up with Lisa as witches, while serving Wicked Witch's brew (apple juice) to the trick-or-treaters.

Margaret often helped at Lisa's school (typically PTA types of things) and performed some of Peg's radio sketches on stage with Lisa.

Margaret's correspondence to Lisa
"Pumpkin Pie" after visiting the Lynch family on Halloween

Margaret, Lisa, and Peg Lynch doing a radio sketch at Lisa's school

Peg Lynch, daughter Lisa, and Margaret

After moving to her Gramercy Park apartment in the mid-50s (right around the corner from Peg), they formed an informal women's social club that met on Sunday evenings at Margaret's place. The "Sunday Night Ladies Club" consisted of women in the entertainment field from stage, screen, radio, and television. Margaret would usually prepare a light supper, and the gals would bring a side dish as they chatted about the latest show business happenings over food and drinks.

Some of the regular attendees of the Sunday evening gatherings included twice nominated Academy Award actress Mildred Dunnock (also a resident in Margaret's Gramercy Park building); actress and regular panelist on TV's *What's My Line* Arlene Francis; Primetime Emmy Award winner Mildred Natwick; Helen Hayes, the first woman to have won an Emmy, a Grammy, an Oscar, and a Tony Award (EGOT); Evie Juster; and Agnes DeMille, among others.

Working on *Ethel and Albert* (and its various incarnations) aside, the bulk of Margaret's career moving forward consisted of many short-lived bit roles in television, movies, regional theater, radio, and the occasional coveted Broadway performance. Although there were a few exceptions, such as her Cora commercials and the year-long tour of *A*

Little Night Music, most later opportunities did not offer long-term prospects.

Some of the minor roles occurred in several soap operas over the years, along with appearing on talk shows (Dick Cavett, Merv Griffin, Johnny Carson, and David Frost, among others). The talk show hosts loved her lively personality, plus the fact that she'd inevitably talk about *The Wizard of Oz.*

In one unique twist, Margaret reprised a role on stage that she did during the early days of television. After playing the holier-than-though Mrs. Dudgeon in *The Devil's Disciple* on television in 1955, she would repeat the role many times over the years. Following her television portrayal,

Margaret performed in *The Devil's Disciple* on a 1958 summer tour, at 1970's American Shakespeare Festival in Stratford, Connecticut, and in 1978 at both Los Angeles and New York among many locations.

Margaret as Mrs. Dudgeon in *The Devil's Disciple*

Describing her performance at the American Shakespeare Festival, *Harvard Crimson* Theater Critic Caldwell Titcomb stated, "The play proper introduces us first to Mrs. Dudgeon, the one thoroughly unpleasant and unsympathetic person Shaw ever fashioned. Through her, Shaw was attacking what he viewed as the worst aspects of organized religion. In this production, the role is in the capable hands of Margaret Hamilton."

As the 1950s drew to a close, Margaret continued to juggle her many acting jobs and got the chance to be in not one – but TWO Christmas specials.

In the 1958 *Hallmark Hall of Fame* television show "The Christmas Tree," Margaret and Jessica Tandy played two ladies running an orphanage in a segment entitled "Miracle in the Orphanage."

Richard Thomas, best known as John Boy of *The Waltons*, made his television premiere playing an orphan. He shared with Adrienne Faillace from the Television Academy how Jessica and Margaret "were wonderful to me. The idea of working very early on with older actors — from whom you obviously had a great deal to learn —

this is part of the great thing about being a child actor. You're apprenticing. You're learning all the time."

TODAY'S TV
Stars Glitter on 'Christmas Tree'

Seven stars, five of whom have current Broadway roles, are featured in the cast of "The Christmas Tree," a special holiday program on "Hallmark Hall of Fame" tonight at 7 on Channel 3. It's in color.

Helen Deutsch wrote the script for the hour-long program, featuring Ralph Bellamy, Carol Channing, Maurice Evans, Tom Poston, Cyril Ritchard, William Shatner and Jessica Tandy.

Here are the highlights—

Miss Channing and Ritchard team up for an ice skating pantomime, "Christmas Day in the Park."

Evans appears in a Nativity scene based on the Biblical chapters of Matthew and Luke.

Miss Tandy and Margaret Hamilton appear in a short drama, "The Miracle of the Orphanage."

Bellamy and Shatner act in another short teleplay, "Light One Candle."

Richard Thomas (John Boy from *The Waltons*)
made his television debut with Margaret in *The Christmas Tree*

[246]

And the following year, in 1959, Margaret appeared in another holiday special, *Once Upon A Christmas Time*. The heartwarming television show is about the citizens of a Vermont village wanting to open their homes to the town's orphans for Christmas.

Margaret, channeling her inner Scrooge or perhaps Miss Gulch, plays the mean orphanage director, Miss Scugg, who initially rebuffs their efforts. Among the cast members were Claude Rains, singer Kate Smith, and a young Patty Duke, who portrayed one of the orphans. A *Variety* review of the program noted, "The show rose above the usual sentimental Christmas fare by virtue of its musical and ice-skating numbers."

Patty Duke and Claude Rains in *Once Upon a Christmas Time*

12

BROADWAY AND A SONG (OR TWO)

Margaret sought roles wherever they were available if she was free. But her first love was and always remained performing on the stage – especially on the Broadway stage. During the 1950s, Margaret was able to perform in several Broadway shows sandwiched around her various television, radio, and commercial endeavors.

Fancy Meeting You Again premiered at Broadway's Royal Theatre in January 1952 and was marketed as a comedic play centered on a woman's attempt to convince her lover to marry her. In what would be her first Broadway play since moving back to New York City, Margaret played Lucy Bascomb, an acidulous secretary. *The New York Times* gave Margaret a nice review, stating she "gives an entertaining performance in a familiar style." Despite her positive review, the play flopped and lasted less than a week, much to Margaret's disappointment.

Margaret's next Broadway play was *Diary of a Scoundrel* at the Phoenix Theatre in November 1956 and had only a slightly better outcome than *Fancy Meeting You Again*. The play was about one man's attempt to manipulate his way into upper-class Russian society in the 19th century, no matter what it takes. Margaret played Madame Kleopatra Mamaeva, a Russian high society matron, and the production featured a stellar cast that included a young Roddy McDowall, comedienne extraordinaire Jerry Stiller, and Peter Falk (of *Columbo* fame) making his Broadway debut. Despite the multi-talented cast, the play received less than complimentary reviews in the New York press and lasted only a month.

Margaret Hamilton with Roddy McDowall in *Diary of a Scoundrel*

Goldilocks was Margaret's third and final Broadway play of the 1950s. Though the production had less than sparkling reviews, it did last for four months – a far better fate than Margaret's previous two Broadway plays that decade. Not to be confused with the children's fairytale with a similar name, *Goldilocks* was a nostalgic romantic comedy – and it was also Margaret's first musical on Broadway (the other one being the aforementioned short-lived 1969 flop *Come Summer* with Ray Bolger).

Goldilocks was noteworthy for Margaret in that she got to sing in the production – one of her overlooked talents. Over her lengthy career, Margaret only sang a few times in her many appearances. On the few occasions when she sang (mostly in stage performances), there was no musical recording of the production. *Goldilocks* is an exception, and Margaret is featured in two songs: "Bad Companions" and "Two Years in the Making" on the soundtrack.

Two other rare opportunities where you can listen to Margaret sing in movies are in 1940's *The Villain Still Pursued Her* and in 1970's *Brewster McCloud*. In *The Villain Still Pursued Her*, Margaret sings "My Bonnie" for a brief couple of stanzas, and her contralto voice is quite charming. In *Brewster McCloud*, Margaret belts out an over-the-top version of "The Star-Spangled Banner" – and the movie's soundtrack includes the song.

Margaret's surprising singing ability can be attributed to her years of formal voice and diction lessons in Cleveland with renowned singing instructor Grace Probert. Cynthia Ware, a student of Grace Probert from Lakewood (near Cleveland), explained her technique of using a cork to relax the lower jaw and minimize the Midwestern pronunciation of the letter "r." It is a good assumption that Margaret undertook similar training with Miss Probert.

Margaret acknowledged in multiple interviews that Grace Probert was the person who motivated her to follow a path in theater despite initially yielding to her parents' preference for her to go to kindergarten training school.

Grace Probert
Teacher of Singing
(Old Italian Method)
Studio, 217-218 The Clarence Bldg.
Pupil of Aglaja Orgeni, Dresden, Germany; Pauline Viardot, Paris, France; Frida De Gebele Ashforth, New York City.

Early 20th century Cleveland advertisement

In a 1982 Cinekyd (youth media program) television interview, Margaret spoke whimsically to the gathered audience how her singing teacher once shared, 'that my voice is coming on very well, though you could never sing opera" and I said, "Miss Probert, I don't want to sing opera!" Margaret described how Miss Probert said several nice things about her singing and how she could make a nice career of it.

Margaret's singing talent was highlighted in her early vaudevillian solo performance called *Heartrending and*

Humorous Songs of 1840, 1890, and 1929, as explained in Chapter 3.

Other plays in which Margaret displayed her singing talents included the 1956 and 1966 revivals of *Show Boat* (as Parthy Anne Hawks); *Annie, Get Your Gun* (as Dolly Tate); in the 1969 Broadway revival, *Oklahoma!* as Aunt Eller; *A Little Night Music* as Madame Armfeldt on tour; and 1950's short-lived *Little Boy Blue* (closed in less than a week).

Margaret in *Show Boat* at Lincoln Center in New York 1966

Margaret as Aunt Eller in *Oklahoma!*

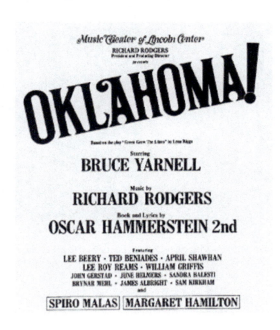

Singing roles aside, Margaret had a couple more Broadway shows, including one that was a major flop. 1966's U.T.B.U lasted less than a week and featured Tony Randall in a truly bizarre play. The story was about a blind man who belongs to a secret society called U.T.B.U. (Unhealthy To Be Unpleasant), whose mission is to rid the world of unpleasant people by blowing them up with specially-made bombs disguised as music boxes.

Thelma Ritter, Margaret, and Tony Randall in *U.T.B.U*

Luckily, Margaret's final show on the Broadway stage was the highly successful 1969 revival of *Our Town* with her friend Hank (Henry) Fonda, as detailed in Chapter 5.

It should be noted that there was an additional Broadway show Margaret was supposed to be in that never materialized. The Broadway debut of *Tattered Tom,* based on the Horatio Alger novel, was scheduled for spring 1970. *Tattered Tom* would have featured an exceptional cast, which included Debbie Reynolds and Robert Alda, known for his role as Sky Anderson in the original New York production of *Guys and Dolls*. The music was to be composed by the duo of Hugh Martin and Ralph Blane, who collaborated on the songs of *Meet Me in St. Louis.*

Margaret was to play "granny," the female heavy in *Tattered Tom*, who is the guardian of a young female street urchin. "It's a fun part, sort of a lady Fagin[5] - full of ginger!" is how Margaret described the part to her friend Wes Wehr. A combination of problems led to the show never happening.

---

[5] Fagin is the old scoundrel in *Oliver Twist* who teaches young orphans to be pickpockets

Tattered Tom never made it to Broadway

Throughout the early 1960s, Margaret prioritized her theatrical performances over sporadic appearances in television and film. She received modest publicity for appearing as a spinster in two episodes of *Car 54, Where Are in You?* in 1963, and as a housekeeper twice on *The Patty Duke Show*.

One TV show Margaret enjoyed doing several times was *The Shari Lewis Show,* appearing in three episodes as herself. The children's show featured Shari (a ventriloquist) playing with several puppets in fun and educational skits, which Margaret enjoyed as she loved children so much.

Unfortunately, Shari's daughter Mallory recalled meeting Margaret as a young child and how terrified she was. Talking with Anthony Taylor from *ATL Retro*, Mallory shared the story of how, as a child, "I was terrified of *The Wizard of Oz*. It was the scariest movie on the planet. I came into my house, and Margaret Hamilton, the woman who played the Wicked Witch, was sitting in the living room. I took one look at her and screamed and went running upstairs."

Shari Lewis with Lambchop and Hushpuppy

Margaret received far more notoriety than she had in years when she appeared in several episodes of the popular *Addams Family* television show as Morticia Addams' mother, Hester Frump. Not only did she appear on the show, but unlike her typical minor role, there was an actual episode dedicated to her titled "Happy Birthday Grandma Frump."

In this *Addams Family* episode, their children find an old photo album that includes a photo of a young Granny Frump. "A dazzler!" states Gomez Addams, referring to her photo. When the Addams' kids wish that Granny could be pretty again, Morticia comes up with the idea of sending her to Barbara Benson's Beauty Farm as a birthday present.

Well, Grandma Frump comes to the mistaken conclusion that Morticia and Gomez plan to ship her off to an old folks' home instead. The comedy ensues as Granny Frump tries to show everyone she's still "full of vim and vigor" and isn't yet ready to be put away.

Gomez Addams and Grandma Frump in the episode "Happy Birthday Grandma Frump"

Margaret's role as Grandma Frump aligned perfectly with her becoming a grandmother to Chris and Scott Meserve a couple of years later. Margaret's experience with having new grandkids was bittersweet, as she had limited chances to see them (and later her granddaughter Margaret) grow up. As noted previously, her only son Ham and his family lived overseas for more than a decade, with his occupation as an international banker.

Around the same time in the 1960s, Margaret's older brother Edwin passed away, followed by the death of her older sister Dorothy a couple of years later in 1968. Losing Dorothy was especially tough on Margaret. The two sisters had remained close with Dorothy, living in Bridgehampton, just a couple of hours away in New York, and the two often visited each other and took vacations together.

Despite these personal tragedies, Margaret always stayed upbeat and never lost her sense of humor.

One time, Margaret was in Palm Beach playing the role of a maid in *Old Acquaintance* when she devised an amusing prank. In her typical maid attire, she joined the hired help at a ritzy Palm Beach party hosted by her friend Mrs. L.E. Marron and served the guests drinks. *LOOK Magazine* learned about the caper and noted some guests "thought they recognized her, but she assured them in a thick Irish brogue, 'Everyone says her and I look alike.' Then she would add, 'But I'm the pretty one.'"

There was another occasion when Margaret's great sense of humor was clearly evident, and it occurred during a lunch outing at a restaurant where she was accompanied by her friend Wes Wehr. A day after *The Wizard of Oz* had been on television for its annual showing, restaurant staff kept glancing towards Margaret. Wes noted, "The waitress and the cook kept staring at Margaret, thinking that she looked somehow familiar. Finally, the waitress said, 'Excuse me, but has anyone ever told you that you look like that actor Margaret Hamilton?' Margaret laughed, 'Yes, I have heard that before.' 'Have you ever *met* her?' the waitress asked. 'Yes, I have,' Margaret answered. 'And quite frankly, dear, I was not particularly impressed by her.'" The next time Wes visited the restaurant, he passed along personal greetings from Margaret to the staff.

13
THE KINDEST OF WITCHES

Author and friend Aljean Harmetz fondly referred to Margaret Hamilton as "the kindest of witches." Margaret's renowned hospitality, helping with many good causes, and her unending commitment to answering every child's letter who wrote to her was amazing. To this day, countless fans have shared treasured memories of her and their letter keepsakes.

Former Beverly Hills neighbor and family friend Bill Marx (son of comedian Harpo Marx) spoke warmly about staying with Margaret at her Gramercy Park apartment when he spent his first Christmas away from home in New York City. Finding his way in a new city and a new career in music, Margaret provided Bill with a wonderful holiday and a pleasant reminder about his former life back home in Beverly Hills.

Up-and-coming artist Wesley Wehr met Margaret at a party in Seattle when she was performing there at the Seattle Repertory Theatre as Mrs. Malaprop in *The Rivals* in

1968. The two of them quickly bonded and became fast friends. Wesley recounted how when he visited her in 1969, she invited him to use her Gramercy Park apartment, giving him the key to the residence. She told him, "Sometimes people in New York can be somewhat snobbish. Please feel free to give my Gramercy Park apartment as your New York address. It's a good address to have here."

34 Gramercy Park, New York City

Margaret may even have been too hospitable occasionally, as shared by her son Hamilton Meserve in a presentation he did about her at a 2015 Judy Garland Museum convention. Ham noted how he and his wife Helen, early in their marriage, were living with his mother, who often allowed out-of-work homeless actors to sleep in her apartment at night. Ham and his wife recalled how they often had to step over the bodies sleeping on the floor of her small apartment.

Another great example of how accommodating Margaret was to everyone, especially younger folks, occurred in the late 1970s. As an aspiring high school journalism student, Carl Anthony was pleasantly surprised when he was able to visit Margaret Hamilton near Halloween and interview her about her life and career for his high school newspaper, *The Verdict*. Carl described how, before they began the interview in her Gramercy Park apartment, Margaret said, "she had a surprise" for him and got some coffee cake (or as she called it, "monkey bread") from the kitchen. After eating some of the coffee cake, Carl politely remarked that it was a bit dry, and Margaret then proceeded to get him a glass of water. Carl joked, "I thought you were going to bring me a cup of Maxwell House!" as she was still doing her commercials as Cora for them. To which she replied, "I don't drink that!"

As Carl began the interview, Margaret gave some background information on her early years as a kindergarten teacher in Cleveland, Ohio. He tried some more humor, as you might expect from a high school kid, and commented slyly, "So you were the Wicked Witch of the Midwest before you were the Wicked Witch of the West?" But apparently, she didn't think it was that funny. Margaret then elaborated on her career in the theater, movies, television, and ultimately *The Wizard of Oz*.

Carl admitted droning on a bit too long with some items, and before he knew it, she had fallen asleep – for quite a while, as it would turn out. Carl said he wasn't quite sure what to do and devilishly flashed back to the scene of the witch getting splashed in the face with the water, but no, he couldn't do that and instead just yelled loudly a couple of times, "Mrs. Hamilton! Mrs. Hamilton!" to which she finally woke up, a bit embarrassed and apologetic. She even gave Carl a couple of autographed photos at the end of his visit and thanked him for his patience.

Margaret's signed photo to Carl
(including her "thanks for your patience" note)

In the Grammercy Park apartment building, resident Susan Tunick expressed how Margaret fittingly helped start a Halloween tradition there. "This fine woman (Margaret) helped to create a yearly tradition at 34 Gramercy Park." Susan described how the winding hallways "were filled with candle-lit pumpkins and baskets of goodies" and that "one year we were there, Margaret Hamilton hung her Wicked Witch costume in the doorway and greeted the youngsters as they rang the bell."

Besides Margaret sending hundreds of letters to her young fans over the years, she was also a prolific writer to many of her close friends. Libraries in Seattle and New York City store some of her voluminous correspondences. In Minnesota, the Linden Hill Estate in Little Falls, Minnesota, hosted an exhibit about *The Wizard of Oz* featuring a sizable number of items from Margaret Hamilton to friend and heiress Laura Jane Musser.

Laura's relative, Peter Miller Musser, was an investor in *The Wizard of Oz* movie, so she was fortunate enough to be able to visit the movie set. Margaret and Laura formed a fast friendship during Laura's visits. In turn, Margaret visited the Linden Hill Estate several times and went on vacations with Laura. She also stayed in touch with Laura through frequent correspondence, some of which is showcased in a Linden Hill Estate exhibit.

Laura shared many of the same interests as Margaret and, through her philanthropy, set up The Laura Jane Musser Fund to continue with some of her interests in life, including the arts and helping children.

Margaret and Laura Jane Musser

The autographed photo below to Laura is from the Linden Hill Estate's *Wizard of Oz* exhibit featuring many Margaret Hamilton items.

Transcribed text in the photo from Margaret to Laura Jane Musser: "I am hiding in hopes of seeing Laura Jane Musser pop along in her usual way, but so far, no luck. Only the scarecrow and Dorothy, but it's a little bit of luck."

- Margaret Hamilton

Even with her busy schedule, Margaret always found time to support several causes. She volunteered with the Veterans Bedside Network at several New York City hospitals. Founded in 1948, the Veterans Bedside Network was based on an interesting concept in which hospitalized veterans wrote scripts for shows and then directed and acted in them. Margaret, with her show business background, fit right in and enjoyed helping with this unique therapeutic activity.

And from her days with the Junior League of Los Angeles, Margaret was lauded in the League's 85th Anniversary Issue for "the program of Educational Therapy she outlined and put into execution at the (Children's) Convalescent Home in Los Angeles." The program consisted of storytelling, games, music, and crafts therapy designed to help young children thrive to the best of their ability.

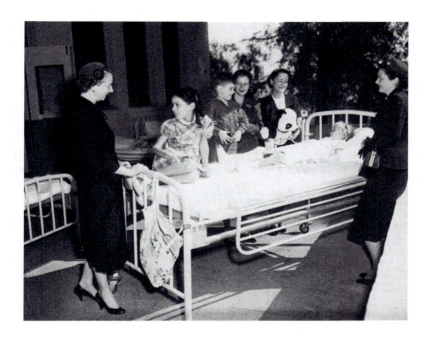

Junior League members at the Los Angeles Convalescent Home

Another of Margaret's passions was being an animal rights advocate. She volunteered with the Friends of Animals organization and also did some public service announcements for spaying and neutering your pets.

Related to her animal rights advocacy, she spoke out on behalf of the severe fishing practices in the tuna industry that were needlessly killing porpoises in fishing nets that were supposed to just be for catching tuna.

Wicked witch is a softie when it comes to plight of porpoises

Actress Margaret Hamilton, best known as Cora the TV coffee lady, is brewing up a campaign to stop the slaughter of gentle dolphins.

The beloved 78-year-old actress who has appeared in 70 movies since her debut as the Wicked Witch of the West in "The Wizard of Oz," is outraged over the killing of thousands of the graceful sea mammals every year.

"Every time I think about one of these gentle porpoises being caught up in tuna fishing nets, I run the gamut of emotion from great sadness to extreme outrage," Miss Hamilton said.

"Over the next five years, the Department of Commerce will allow fishermen to kill more than 20,000 porpoises a year — 102,500 over half a decade.

"They are overriding the advice and warnings of their own scientists.

"No one understands why the porpoise kill to approach zero by 1974.

"Twenty thousand dead porpoises a year is far from zero," said the actress who has given long hours of her time to the speech-making and letter-writing campaign to save porpoises.

"Other people ask me why I'm so concerned about saving animals. They say humans are important.

"Sure, they are, but what we do to animals, especially gentle porpoises, is so degrading to the human race.

"It takes a porpoise a half hour to die after they're caught in one of these huge nets and the experience is one of excruciating terror for the whole family.

"They have very close families and when a mother sees her pup get caught, she tries to rescue him and the aunts and uncles and everybody else gets caught up in it, too, and then they all drown.

"Porpoises are the finest

Margaret Hamilton — the Maxwell House coffee lady, Cora, on TV and the Wicked Witch of the West in "The

Margaret advocating on behalf of the porpoises

Another organization Margaret helped was the Episcopal Actors' Guild. Their mission is "to provide emergency aid and support to professional performers of all faiths and those who are undergoing financial crisis. We are also dedicated to helping emerging artists advance their careers through scholarships, awards, and performance opportunities."

Margaret told the *Gramercy Herald* how the Guild's Executive Director, Lorraine Sherwood, "asked if I would join the board and I became terribly interested in it. And it feels that the Guild is a good cause to which she is able to contribute." The article further noted that Margaret once conducted a memorial service at the church for departed actors and lent her services to serve as a chairperson for a Guild fundraising benefit. "You just lend your name and put on your best party dress – Miss Sherwood does everything – but it's nice to know that you can help."

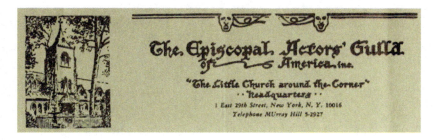

On a lighter note, as much as Margaret enjoyed shopping at the iconic toy store FAO Schwarz, she enjoyed even more doing special holiday readings at the store for both Christmas and Halloween.

Perhaps there was no cause more passionate to Margaret than when she took part with many noted authors in the April 1982 "An Evening of Banned Books" censorship event sponsored by PEN America, the writers' association. The event dramatized the various speakers' opposition to censorship by staging a public reading of various banned books at Manhattan's Public Theater. Among those reading some famous and forbidden lines were John Irving, Arthur Schlesinger, Erica Jong, E. L. Doctorow – and Margaret Hamilton.

Arranged by and accompanied by her close friend and noted Oz author, Michael Patrick Hearn, Margaret needed little urging to speak out against the past censorship of her favorite book since childhood – *The Wonderful Wizard of Oz*.

Margaret described sternly in the PEN video of the event how the book *The Wonderful Wizard of Oz*, "was first banned from many public library systems in the 1920s, most children's librarians feeling 'that the Oz books had nothing of worth to offer to young readers.'" She added, "In 1957, the Director of the Detroit Public Library System banned *The Wonderful Wizard of Oz* for negativism and for generally being of no value."

Time Magazine reported, "Book censorship is like them taking a book out of my own home," huffed Hamilton, something of an American classic herself.

Margaret then read a chapter from *The Wonderful Wizard of Oz*, much to the delight of the audience.

A passionate Margaret Hamilton reads *The Wonderful Wizard of Oz*

Margaret and Michael Patrick Hearn would also go to The University of Connecticut at Storrs once or twice a year to speak at Prof. Francelia Butler's Children's

Literature Class. Prof. Butler, like Margaret, hailed from the Cleveland area and was a close friend of hers. Terri Goldich from the U Conn's Children's Literature Collection said, "Butler's courses on children's literature were among the most popular on campus. Celebrated figures such as esteemed baby doctor Benjamin Spock, *Sesame Street's* Big Bird, and actress Margaret Hamilton, who played the Wicked Witch of the West in the film *The Wizard of Oz*, were recruited to speak to her classes."

Margaret Hamilton and Michael Patrick Hearn at U Conn

Margaret was always generous to a fault, accommodating requests for her time. She rarely turned down an invitation to appear at an event, whether it was an Oz-themed convention or being a guest of honor at an event, such as the Sons of the Desert Christmas Party.

Sons of the Desert defines itself as "devoted to keeping the lives and works of Stan Laurel and Oliver Hardy before the public, and to have a good time while doing it." The group takes its name from a lodge that the comedians belong to in the 1933 film *Sons of the Desert*. Following the whimsical "desert" theme, the society's local chapters are affectionately known as "tents" and named after iconic Laurel & Hardy films.

And Margaret was a member of the group, as it tapped into her joy of comedy.

Ray Cabana Jr. shared a touching story about Margaret's appearance as a special Christmas guest at a 1980s Ladies Night event for The Sons of the Desert in the Connecticut Valley chapter of the organization. Ray noted how his friend, Hal Stanton, the Grand Vizier of the "tent" (local chapter), "asked members of the audience, given Miss Hamilton's arthritis, that fans request no more than one autograph," and audience members politely obliged.

Later, Ray had time to talk with Margaret after the event in a booth of a nearby restaurant, and an employee (possibly the manager) "came over with a stack of the restaurant menus and asked the former actress to sign each and every one of them. I literally heard her sigh. But then she said with a hint of reluctance as she commenced signing the menu, 'Oh well, I guess I should be pleased that people want them.' Such was this wonderful individual!"

Many of Margaret Hamilton's fans have charming stories about meeting her as a child, like the one from author Paul Miles Schneider. Traveling to attend a relative's wedding in New York City, Paul got the surprise of his young life. His grandfather, a former executive at Warner Brothers, arranged for him to have a surprise meeting with Margaret Hamilton, who was also in town, performing in *Oklahoma* at the Lincoln Center.

After going to Margaret's dressing room, Paul described how he met "this sweet little old lady" and recalls just staring at her. She certainly didn't seem mean or frightening or ugly to him, and after Margaret answered several of Paul's questions, he wasn't convinced she was the Wicked Witch of the West, and she could sense it.

Finally, she asked Paul if he believed it was her.

Then she looked at Paul and smiled. "Maybe this will convince you," she said. "Then she laughed. Yes, I mean *the* laugh. That horrific, high-pitched, devious cackle that has caused generations of young children to run terrified from their living room TV sets," Paul shared. He suddenly realized he was indeed in the presence of the Wicked Witch of the West.

Paul never forgot that meeting with Margaret. Two months later, when school started, he began the second grade, and his teacher asked the students to find a pen pal for the year - ideally someone they met over the summer. He proudly announced to his teacher, "I choose the Wicked Witch of the West from *The Wizard of Oz!*"

Paul wrote to Margaret and became her pen pal for the year. He was lucky enough to meet her again years later and considered Margaret to be one of the nicest people he had ever met or known. She was a major influence on him when he later wrote his popular Oz-inspired novel, *Silver Shoes.*

Paul Miles Schneider and his cherished correspondence with Margaret Hamilton

As a youngster, Randy Ward had a fun encounter with Margaret, which he shared. After waiting in a long line to see her at a public appearance, "this little girl with pigtails jumped in line in front of me. So I just grabbed her pigtail and pulled her behind me. Well, when I made it up to Margaret, she was so sweet and answered a couple of questions. Then she asked me to come behind the table and stand by her. I was thrilled! When I got beside her, she whacked me gently on the bottom and said, 'Gentlemen never pull lady's hair.' Then she hugged me and said now I could say I was spanked by The Wicked Witch of the West. I'll never forget that."

Ken Rowe was one of the lucky children who not only corresponded with Margaret but, years later, got to visit her in New York City along with a family friend. Ken recalled, "When I was a child, I recognized Margaret Hamilton on the Maxwell House Coffee TV commercials. She was always my favorite character in *The Wizard of Oz*. I had to get a fan letter to her. Since my parents drank the coffee, I grabbed the jar and got the address for General Foods off the label. I wrote them a letter asking for Miss Hamilton's address, and they sent it to me! That started a correspondence between us that lasted for six years. She wrote back (about a dozen letters over the years, and of course, I still have them!), and she sent me about half a dozen 8x10 glossies with scenes from the movie, all autographed! When I got old enough, I asked her if I could come to NYC to meet her, and she accepted!"

Upon finally getting the chance to meet Margaret as a teenager at her apartment in Gramercy Park, Ken was greeted by her with open arms and a warm, "Kenny, it's so nice to finally meet you, dear." After a friendly hug,

Ken was able to take some photos, and described how Margaret "pulled out her scrapbook of photos (huge thrill) and told a couple of stories."

"Then, Miss Hamilton took us to her favorite restaurant, Lüchow's, which was just a short walk away. We sat at a table in the center of the restaurant and soon noticed that people were pointing. One girl walked over and asked for an autograph. I was just a young teenager and felt so important to be sitting with Miss Hamilton. She topped off the day by giving me and my buddy two tickets to the hottest show on Broadway back then, *Annie*. My trip was brief, but I felt like I had visited Oz when I got back home to black and white Virginia. The next day, I sent Miss Hamilton flowers to thank her for the thrill of my young life. What a grand lady!"

An autographed photo Margaret sent to Ken Rowe, commanding one of her flying monkeys to "Bring Me Kenny!"

Margaret was never too busy to accommodate her fans.

Margaret Hamilton – the kindest witch

14

THERE'S NO PLACE LIKE HOME - PART 2

Even though she spent a good portion of her life living in California and later New York City, Margaret always remained fond of her hometown of Cleveland. Between occasional visits to appear again at The Cleveland Play House and attend other special events, Margaret was always accommodating to the people from her birthplace. Her trips to Cleveland typically included a visit to her old high school, Hathaway Brown, along with seeing hometown friends and relatives.

In 1965-66, The Cleveland Play House celebrated its 50th Anniversary Season, and Margaret was invited to be a part of the festivities. In October 1965, Margaret Hamilton wowed audiences and critics alike with her portrayal in Moliere's *Tartuffe*, earning high praise from Cleveland theater critic Peter Bellamy.

Publicity photo of Margaret Hamilton for her 1965
Cleveland Play House appearance in *Tartuffe*

Margaret returned in early 1967 to help The Cleveland Play House get the new year off to a great start. She appeared as Madame Arcati in Noel Coward's *Blithe Spirit*, drawing high praise from *Cleveland Press* theater critic Tony Mastroianni, who described Margaret's performance as "the dotty spiritualist dominates the play. But Miss Hamilton goes beyond mere domination. She has taken on complete ownership."

Mastroianni went into great detail about Margaret's amazing performance: "Hers is a stare that withers, a retort that snaps, a cliché-filled dialog that emerges as a string of freshly coined phrases."

"Observe her in her moment of triumph, stomping across the stage, her handkerchief fluttering like a battle flag. Notice as her eyes narrow and then widen, as her lips purse, as her hands move – tellingly, but economically. She has flawless timing and the quick sureness that allows her to cover another actor's fumble."

Ruth McDevitt and Margaret Hamilton
in Noel Coward's *Blithe Spirit*

Celebrating Margaret's 1967 return to Cleveland for *Blithe Spirit*

Another way Margaret stayed connected with her Cleveland and Ohio roots was through performing with the Kenley Players. They were a pioneering summer stock company that presented countless productions with stars from Broadway, film, and TV in Midwestern cities from 1940 to 1996. The Kenley circuit involved performances in Akron, Warren, Dayton, Cleveland, Columbus, and occasionally, other cities outside Ohio.

Recalling his experiences with Margaret and the Kenley Players, Edward Burlando shared, "We were both actors in summer stock, where we did several plays together, including *The Man Who Came to Dinner* in 1968. I have never met another actor as kind and sweet as she was. We used to talk and eat sandwiches together during our breaks in the Kenley Players."

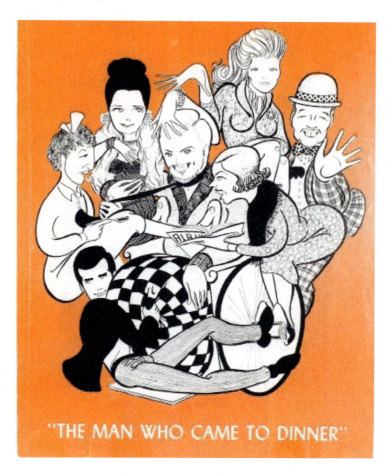

1968 Kenley Players playbill featuring Margaret Hamilton and Jack Cassidy (a caricature of Margaret on the left)

What would have been one of the epic theatrical lineups of all time involving Margaret and the Kenley Players never happened. In 1973, the Kenley Players were planning to do a reprisal of *Arsenic and Old Lace* that included William Shatner, Lon Chaney Jr., and Margaret that would tour several Ohio cities. Captain Kirk, the Wolf Man, and the Wicked Witch of the West – all together. Sadly, a month before the start of the production, Lon Chaney Jr. unexpectedly passed away. Making matters worse, Margaret also had to bow out because of some personal schedule conflicts.

Original *Arsenic and Old Lace* early ad from May

Revised *Arsenic and Old Lace* ad published before the actual show (without Margaret and Lon Chaney Jr.)

During the 1970s, Margaret made several trips back to Ohio. In October 1975, she returned to help celebrate The Cleveland Play House's 60th anniversary. Included in the anniversary festivities was making Margaret an honorary trustee of the Play House. She was only the fifth person in 60 years to receive such an honor. The others who received the honor were Joel Grey, Helen Hayes, Lillian Gish, and Katharine Cornell.

Margaret with Cleveland Play House Director Richard Oberlin

Margaret also accepted the challenge of being chairperson for the first national alumni fund-raising campaign for The Cleveland Play House in 1977. Along with members of the national alumni committee – Dom DeLuise, Jerome Lawrence, Robert E. Lee, and Jack Weston – Margaret undertook the challenge of helping to raise the funds that would help sustain the theater's unique place in the city of Cleveland's Arts Community.

To achieve "All-American City"[6] status, the "New Cleveland Campaign" began in the late 1970s. Cleveland asked for the support of its current and former residents in the campaign, and Margaret was more than willing to assist.

"New Cleveland Campaign" newspaper advertisement featuring Margaret with a *Wizard of Oz* theme

---

[6] The National Civic League's All-American City Award recognizes 10 communities each year for their civic accomplishments and innovative approaches to addressing issues.

Margaret was the recipient of a 1977 Governor's Award from her home state of Ohio. The Governor's Award is presented to "Ohio men and women from all walks of life and are awarded plaques, testifying to their contributions to the world and the respect that the Buckeye State has for those accomplishments." The ceremony for the 1977 winners took place in Columbus, Ohio, in February 1978, presided over by Gov. James A. Rhodes.

Governor James A. Rhodes

Ohio Governor's Award recipients that evening included restaurateur Bob Evans, Cleveland business executive and New York Yankees owner George Steinbrenner, and country western star Johnny Paycheck, who delighted the crowd with a few bars from his anthemic "Take This Job and Shove It." However, the biggest ovation was reserved for Margaret Hamilton.

Fellow 1977 Ohio Governor's Award recipients (top left going clockwise) George Steinbrenner, Johnny Paycheck, and Bob Evans

Margaret returned to the Cleveland Play House for one last performance in Emlyn William's thriller *Night Must Fall* during the 1978-79 Season. In the production, she played Mrs. Bramson, a "crotchety hypochondriac marked for death by a sly killer." *Cleveland Press* theater critic Tony Mastroianni described the play as "a model of suspense, a coup for Director Paul Lee as well."

Commemorating Margaret's 1978 return to Cleveland

After the opening of *Night Must Fall*, there was a heart-warming post-theater "Welcome Home Maggie" party thrown in her honor by her Play House compatriots.

Margaret Hamilton's final Cleveland Play House performance in *Night Must Fall*

To celebrate her achievements in the theater, the Margaret Hamilton Scholarship was established for aspiring young actors and actresses at the Cleveland Play House.

On September 24, 2010, The Women's Committee of The Cleveland Play House hosted a "Hall of Fame" luncheon celebration. The Hall of Fame Class of 2010 inductees, chosen by the Heritage Council of The Cleveland Play House, were showcased at the event. Margaret Hamilton (posthumously), Elizabeth Flory Kelly, Shirley Oberlin, Artha Woods, and Kirk Willis were among the inductees. Hall of Fame member Ed Asner was the Guest of Honor. Coincidentally, one of Margaret's last television appearances was on Ed Asner's *Lou Grant* television show.

HALL OF FAME INDUCTION

Invitations have been mailed and the announcement of Hall Of Fame Inductees has been published. We are sooooo excited that our own Shirley Oberlin is among the 2010 Hall Of Fame Inductees. She joins Margaret Hamilton, Elizabeth Flory Kelly (a former member of the Women's Committee Board), Artha Woods and Kirk Willis. There are many previous inductees but this event has "fallen through the cracks" in recent years. Please join us as we revive this tradition and prepare to celebrate annually in the future.

Elijah Ford has been most helpful to the Women's Committee and is often called 'a fixture" of the Play House. Congratulations, Elijah, on your induction as the Heritage Award Recipient.

The Women's Committee is hosting the Hall Of Fame Luncheon on September 24 at Stages restaurant. Please refer to your invitation and choose the level of participation most comfortable for you. Most of you will remember "Lou Grant" of the Mary Tyler More TV era, WELL, Ed Asner, Cleveland Play House Hall Of Fame Member is our Guest of Honor. This is your opportunity to see Mr. Asner "up close and personal".

2010 CPH Hall of Fame Induction Announcement

Margaret and Ed Asner on the *Lou Grant* TV show

In what is truly a hidden Cleveland gem, you can find Margaret, as the Wicked Witch of the West, along with many other local Cleveland celebrities in the epic "Love Letter to Cleveland" mural by Cleveland artists Gary and

Laura Dumm. Located on the third floor outside the Office of Special Collections in The Michael Schwartz Library at Cleveland State University, Cleveland icons Ghoulardi, Dick Goddard, and Michael Symon surround Margaret in this portion of the mural.

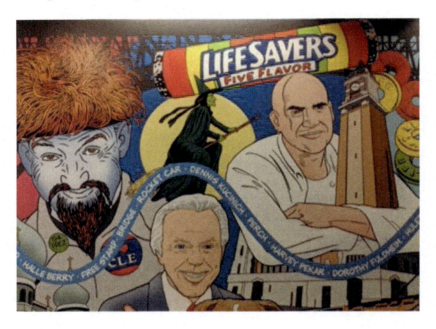

Margaret Hamilton in "Love Letter to Cleveland"

Created in 2013 as a public art project and located in Cleveland's Ohio City neighborhood, "Love Letter to Cleveland" was moved indoors because of the negative impact the weather was having on the quality of the mural's appearance.

And finally, when in Margaret's hometown of Cleveland, there's no better way to celebrate her Oz connection than to visit the aptly named "Flying Monkey Pub" in the city's Tremont neighborhood.

As the hometown *Plain Dealer* reported 20+ years ago, "Walk into the Flying Monkey, the new bar at 819 Jefferson Street in Tremont, and your first thought is: Wow, what a lot of good wood. But where's the monkey? It doesn't take long to find out. Above the bar is a large lacquered box. At the touch of a button, controlled by the bartender, the doors open, and a flying monkey, a smaller version of the ones in *The Wizard of Oz*, comes screaming out of the box."

"'Somewhere after 11 p.m., it's not uncommon to hear chants of *'Show us the monkey,'* says (original) owner Tom Bell. When asked the criteria necessary to see the monkey, he says, 'It's pretty much on request.'"

Modeled after the monkeys from L. F. Baum's *The Wonderful Wizard of Oz* books, the pub and its resident flying monkey have delighted visitors for years.

"Original" flying monkeys

819 Jefferson Street, Cleveland

15

FINAL TRIP DOWN THE YELLOW BRICK ROAD

As the 1960s drew to a close, Margaret adjusted to life without her sister Dorothy while her son and his family remained overseas. Those realities aside, Margaret kept busy with her acting engagements while continuing to advocate for her many causes. Margaret continued to enjoy summers at her Cape Island, Maine cottage, giving her a well-deserved chance to relax.

Several of the friends she made in later years helped fill the void following her sister Dorothy's passing. Wesley Wehr, Laura Jane Musser, Francelia Butler, Michael Patrick Hearn, and William Windom all spent a good amount of time with Margaret – when she had time.

Margaret's television and movie appearances declined in later years. Several roles received much notoriety, while others have been all but forgotten. It's surprising to learn that she appeared in the little-known 1969 film *Angel in*

My Pocket, starring Andy Griffith. Following the conclusion of *The Andy Griffith Show* in 1968, the show's star explored a career in movies. Channeling the same "down home" personality that was so popular with his television show, Andy played a small-town minister trying to mediate a feud between two parish families. Margaret was cast in the movie as a church busybody, providing comedic relief to the dilemma.

Despite mixed reviews, a low box office, and being largely forgotten, the movie offers great trivia questions: 1) After his successful TV show ended, what was Andy Griffith's next project? 2) Which movie had Andy Griffith and Margaret Hamilton as cast members?

Lee Meriwether, Andy Griffith, Margaret Hamilton, and Ruth McDevitt in *Angel in My Pocket*

The offbeat 1970 film *Brewster McCloud* was significant in that it featured Shelley Duvall in her first movie, along with kindling a close friendship between Margaret and William Windom, who were also in the cast.

Shelley Duvall and Bud Cort in *Brewster McCloud*

Margaret and William Windom's friendship blossomed once the filming ended. In his memoir, William noted he would take her to The Players, an exclusive theater and arts club near Margaret's Gramercy Park apartment. And there was also the occasional trip for the two of them to The Russian Tea Room by Carnegie Hall.

1971's *The Anderson Tapes* is a crime movie starring Sean Connery, in which Margaret is a mere blip on the screen as a building tenant. The film is significant, however, because it features what most consider to be the breakout performance of a very young Christopher Walken and is also Margaret's last big screen appearance.

Christopher Walken in *The Anderson Tapes*

Margaret's most publicized television appearances in the 1970s were on *Mister Rogers Neighborhood* and *Sesame Street,* along with her Maxwell House commercials as Cora. A couple of other shows she appeared on that got a decent amount of promotion were *The Partridge Family* and the TV movie *The Night Strangler*. On *The Partridge Family,* she played the mother of the band's promoter Reuben Kincaid. Coincidentally, Ray Bolger appeared on the show, playing the father of Mrs. Patridge (Shirley Jones).

Margaret in *The Partridge Family*

Margaret received accolades as Professor Crabwell, a college expert with a knowledge of the occult in 1973's *The Night Strangler*. She enjoyed playing the role of an educator, which was not too far from her days as a kindergarten teacher. *The Night Strangler* was a sequel to the drama/horror television series *Kolchak: The Night Stalker* starring Darren McGavin, best known for playing Ralphie Parker's father in *A Christmas Story*.

Margaret as Professor Crabwell in *The Night Strangler*

Besides her highly popular role as Cora in the Maxwell House commercials, Margaret triumphed in Stephen Sondheim's *A Little Night Music*. The play toured for a year in the mid-seventies. Margaret amazingly played the role of a retired courtesan, Madame Armfeldt, a woman who sings of a lifetime of sexual conquests in "Liaisons." When interviewed by *Hamilton News* reporter Gary Smith, who wondered why Margaret would select such an unusual role, she replied, "Never you mind. It was a chance to wear a gorgeous costume and to work with Jean

Simmons." Margaret indeed received multiple excellent reviews for her portrayal of Madame Armfeldt.

Margaret in *A Little Night* Music

Continuing to stay busy later in the decade, Margaret was happy to perform at the Cape Playhouse once again in 1977's *Night Must Fall*. She was nostalgic about appearing there, harkening back to when she performed in 1930's *Ship Shapes* at the playhouse. Her costar was David McCallum, best known for his roles in *The Man from U.N.C.L.E.* and years later in *NCIS*.

In contrast to her declining acting career in the late 1970s, Margaret remained in high demand for appearances at the increasing number of Oz-themed events. 1979 saw Margaret being invited as the special guest of honor to three Oz-related events, all commemorating the film's 40th anniversary.

In June 1979, Margaret would take part in the Judy Garland Museum's annual festival in Judy's hometown of Grand Rapids, Minnesota. Margaret was the first celebrity guest to attend the Judy Garland Festival and the first cast member of *The Wizard of Oz* to visit Grand Rapids. Margaret was happy to meet with her many fans and share stories about the filming of *The Wizard of Oz*.

Margaret Hamilton visiting with Grand Rapids children in 1979

Also in June 1979, Margaret Hamilton was the guest of honor at the Ozmopolitan Convention of the International Wizard of Oz Club in Castle Park, Michigan, hosted by her friend Laura Jane Musser. Oz Club member Peter Hanff (who'd previously met Margaret) went with Laura Jane to the airport to meet her upon arrival. Peter shared how delightful it was to see Margaret again and took several photos of her related to the event, where she once more shared her tales about *The Wizard of Oz*.

Margaret arriving at Castle Park, Michigan by plane
(dispelling any rumors of flying in via broomstick)

Margaret in the back of Laura Jane Musser's car

Finally, in October 1979, Margaret was the guest of honor at OZ II in Topeka, Kansas, serving as the grand marshal for the event's parade. Signing autographs, especially for her youngest fans, was a priority for her at the event.

Margaret signing autographs at OZ II in Topeka

Into the 1980s, Margaret would appear in only a few minor television roles as her career wound down. Similarly, she made limited public appearances.

One of these few public appearances was a major career highlight for her in September 1981 at the Telluride Film Festival held in Telluride, Colorado. A tribute was held to celebrate the American character actor, where Margaret was honored alongside John Carradine, Elisha Cook Jr., and Woody Strode. The festival showcased the films of the renowned character actors, including an outdoor screening of *The Wizard of Oz*.

TCM film researcher Jeff Stafford, who attended the festival, commented, "One of the festival highlights for me was the 'Character Actors Tribute' that included a panel discussion with John Carradine, Woody Strode, Margaret Hamilton, and Elisha Cook, Jr., all of whom had delightful anecdotes about their career and specific films. Afterward, I was quite moved by the sight of these actors mingling with the festival goers in the streets or just wandering around town like any other visitor."

Photographer Mark Ryan, who attended the festival with his wife, recalled Margaret repeating her "I'll get you and your little dog, too!" line, much to the audience's delight. Mark also remembered Margaret discussing how she regretted being only remembered for her role in *The Wizard of Oz*. She also talked about getting burned during her fiery exit in Munchkinland. Later, Mark asked Margaret if he could photograph her in front of *The Wizard of Oz* poster, and she was happy to oblige. Mark's photos are on the next two pages.

Margaret in front of the Oz poster at the Telluride Film Festival

Margaret onstage with other character actor honorees:
Woody Strode, John Carradine, and Elias Cook Jr.

A few rare public appearances by Margaret occurred in 1982: her "live" studio interview for the youth media production organization Cinekyd, the Manhattan Public Theater book censorship event that she read at, and a July gathering of former RKO Studio Hollywood stars at New York's Russian Tea Room celebrating the donation of its film archives to the University of California.

In December 1982, Margaret celebrated her 80th birthday with a party at New York City's famed Sardi's restaurant in Manhattan's Theater District. Sardi's is famous for its collection of over 1,000 caricatures of entertainers, including Margaret, identified in her sketch as "Maggie." The honored person normally inscribes a note on the drawing, and she whimsically (referring to actually being identified as Maggie), wrote, "After sixty years, it's about time."

Margaret Hamilton's Sardi's caricature

At the birthday party, old friend Peg Lynch noticed how Margaret seemed to initially have a problem recognizing her and another longtime friend, Arlene Francis.

Nearly a year later, in September 1983, the National Film Society organized a "black-tie Hollywood gala" at the Sheraton-Centre Hotel in Manhattan. The event's chief attraction was to feature James Cagney receiving a "50-year career achievement award" alongside other actors like Mildred Natwick, Margaret's close friend. The person selected to present Mildred with her award was, fittingly, Margaret. Margaret made her first public appearance in a while and was greeted with the evening's loudest applause. "I thought I had an award," she quipped to the crowd. She confided in the audience that her reduced public appearances resulted from her declining memory.

Mildred Natwick (left) and Margaret in 1969's Our Town

Good friend Wesley Wehr also noted around that time, "Margaret's memory began to fail her. She was no longer able to perform on the stage or even do bit parts for television. She was no longer able to live alone in her Gramercy Park apartment. Her family arranged for her to be near them (in Dutchess County, New York) in a Connecticut nursing home where they could visit her regularly."

On May 16, 1985, Margaret passed away from a heart attack at Noble Horizons Nursing Home in Salisbury, Connecticut. In memory of Margaret, a memorial took place at The Little Church Around the Corner, where she actively took part in the Episcopal Actors' Guild of America.

16

BEWITCHING LEGACY

The reports regarding Margaret's passing quickly circulated and were covered extensively by all major news outlets.

Included among the many newspaper stories of Margaret's death were several colorful headlines referencing her iconic role as the Wicked Witch of the West in *The Wizard of Oz*. Joking around earlier on more than one occasion, Margaret stated that when she dies, the classic "Ding Dong the Witch is Dead!" Oz song reference ought to be part of the story.

Quotes

"I hope, when I die, someone has the presence of mind to say, 'Ding Dong, the Witch is really dead.'"
— What Margaret Hamilton, who played the Wicked Witch of the West in *The Wizard of Oz*, told a friend. Hamilton, who is also known for Maxwell House coffee commercials, died recently. From *People*

And sure enough, several newspapers whimsically honored Margaret's request to include her "Ding Dong the Witch is Dead" reference from *The Wizard of Oz*.

Ding Dong, the Witch is dead

MARGARET HAMILTON died last week but the Wicked Witch of the West will live forever. "The Wizard of Oz" is one of those rare films that fits together so well — and has been seen so many times by so many people — that it's beyond criticism. That level of perfection is achieved only through the rarest kind of luck, and with the perfect combination of creative people: actors, writers, directors, set designers and all the rest. If any film can be described as an American classic, it's "The Wizard of Oz." In no small part, that's because of Margaret Hamilton.

She was a character actor who worked extensively in movies and television. Though by all accounts she was a warm, personable woman in her private life, on screen as the Wicked Witch, she embodied greed, power and envy gone mad. (Did you ever, even for a split second, doubt her lust for the ruby slippers?) She was a child's nightmare, an adult transformed into a green monster with a cackling laugh that cut straight to the core of your fear. She discovered the power of basic black clothes long before anyone had ever heard of Darth Vader. She could fly; she could see everything that you did; and she might pop up anywhere.

The film would not work without her. She somehow managed to counterbalance four sympathetic, lovable protagonists and one cute dog by having as much dramatic weight as all of them put together. Though her character isn't on screen for that much time, you can't think of the film without remembering her. If she were missing or if the character were handled lightly, the film would be little more than a nice musical for kids. But because she is so believably evil, both as Miss Gulch and as the Witch, the action plays at a higher level. Perhaps the only comparable role in a comparable film is Claude Raines' Capt. Renault in "Casablanca." Neither is the central character, but both of them somehow "finish" the film.

Margaret Hamilton's portrayal of that character is immortal. Her Wicked Witch will live a long as people watch movies. Audiences will al ways be as thrilled, frightened and amazed by he as they first were in 1939 and still are today They'll enjoy every second of it too.

Ding Dong, the Witch is Dead! Long Live th Witch!

Margaret Hamilton as Witch of the West

Ding, Dong, She's Really Dead
That's What Hamilton Wanted Her Obituary To Say

SALISBURY, Conn. (AP) — Margaret Hamilton, the Wicked Witch of the West who melted at the feet of Dorothy in the 1939 film classic *The Wizard of Oz*, died yesterday of an apparent heart attack. She was 82.

The veteran of more than 75 films and scores of plays died at the Noble Horizons nursing home in Salisbury, where she had been in declining health for a year, said Joann Lunning, director of nursing.

She worked as a character actress for more than 50 years, including a five-year run as Cora, the kindly old storekeeper who appeared in commercials for Maxwell House coffee.

But she was best known for Oz. Generations of children thrilled at her depiction of the green-skinned witch, and with each showing of the film on television she received hundreds of letters from young fans.

The celebrity was ironic, for two reasons. She was a former kindergarten teacher and loved children. And she never thought the witch was her best work.

She once said, however: "I hope that when I die, someone has the presence of mind to say, 'Ding, dong, the witch is really dead.'"

Her death leaves Ray Bolger, who played the Scarecrow, as the only surviving major cast member of the film. The others included Judy Garland as Dorothy, Jack Haley as the Tin Man, Bert Lahr as the Cowardly Lion and Billie Burke as Glinda the Good Witch.

In 1973, Hamilton said she had turned down countless offers to recreate the role. "I suppose I've turned down a fortune, too, but I just don't want to spoil the magic. Little children's minds can't cope with seeing a mean witch alive again," she said.

"Many times, I see mothers and little children and the mothers always recognize me as the witch. Often, they say to the kids, 'Don't you know who she is?

She's the witch in the *Wizard of Oz*.' Then the kids look disappointed and say 'But I thought she melted.' It's as though they think maybe I'm going to go back and cause trouble for Dorothy again."

A native of Cleveland, Hamilton first got a taste of the theater in a class production in high school. But she was trained to teach kindergarten, and went on to operate private schools in Cleveland and Rye, N.Y.

But in 1927, she became a member of the Cleveland Play House, which now sponsors a scholarship fund in her name. Her first role was in a play entitled *The Man Who Ate the Popomack*; in three years, she performed 25 roles.

From there, she won a part in *Another Language*, which played for a year on Broadway. She was hired to reprise her role in the film version in 1932, and that was the start of her Hollywood career.

She appeared in *My Little Chickadee* with W.C. Fields and Mae West, *State of the Union*, *A Slight Case of Murder*, *Nothing Sacred* and many others. As recently as 1971, she appeared in *Brews*

(Continued on page 14)
— HAMILTON

Margaret's iconic portrayal of the Wicked Witch of the West inspired several notable endeavors.

ALL THINGS *WICKED*

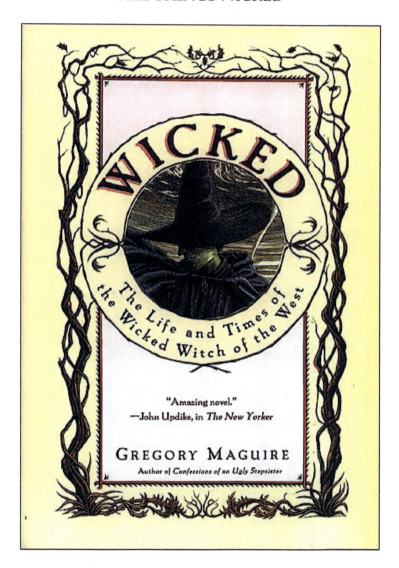

Margaret's frightful role as the Wicked Witch of the West was a factor in creating *Wicked* the novel and its Broadway musical adaptation

Wicked author Gregory Maguire had long been concerned with the nature of good and evil. The aspiring author, hoping to conquer one of the most prevalent themes in entertainment, was conflicted: Could one be born inherently evil?

Maguire noted how "when I realized that nobody had ever written about the second most evil character in the American conscience, the Wicked Witch of the West, I thought I had experienced a small moment of inspiration."

Author Gregory Maguire

While writing *Wicked*, he drank countless cups of Maxwell House coffee in honor of pitchwoman Cora, a.k.a. Margaret Hamilton, a.k.a. the Wicked Witch of the West in the classic film.

Maguire knew Margaret Hamilton's fear-inspiring performance in *The Wizard of Oz* defined the way a witch looked and acted, yet the 1939 movie did not provide a good background for Maguire's "green girl." L. Frank Baum's classic novel, *The Wonderful Wizard of Oz* (written in 1900), never described the Wicked Witch of the West as green – just different.

"I wanted to know why she was different," Maguire said, "so I decided to write about her and create a believable life for Elphaba (the Wicked Witch of the West)." Maguire began writing a prequel to *The Wizard of Oz* movie around the same time Baum's book came out of copyright protection and published *Wicked: The Life and Times of the Wicked Witch of the West* in 1995.

Wicked explores the true personality of Elphaba (derived by shortening the name L. Frank Baum) while reinventing Oz into a land where the boundaries of good and evil are often unclear. Maguire's characters (borrowed or new) have multiple dimensions and present unique alternatives to the contexts offered by *Wicked*'s hybrid sources (the 1939 film and Baum's novels). Glinda (Good Witch of the North), for instance, is not as righteous as depicted in the movie classic.

Reaction to Maguire's novel was strong on both sides of the critical spectrum. Once *Wicked* was released, the author recalls a reporter in Chicago calling the book "heretical." A *New York Times* reporter accused Maguire of abusing a "sacred cow" for his literary advantage. Wicked was wildly popular with most people and remains a bestselling novel today.

Despite all his success, Maguire shared "how he regrets - oh, how he regrets - that he never met Margaret Hamilton." He also regrets more than he can say "that Margaret died before the novel *Wicked* came out." He believes she would have been thrilled by the character's rehabilitation and humanization.

Almost immediately after *Wicked's* release, Marc Platt, a highly successful movie producer for Universal Pictures (*Philadelphia, Legally Blonde*), gained the rights to the novel, intending to create a film version.

"I've been long attracted to characters who are outsiders," Platt said. Naturally, Elphaba fit this description; Platt attempted to write a screenplay for a drama focusing primarily on the Wicked Witch's unstable friendship with Glinda.

Success for most movies requires that the audience easily identify themselves with the characters. "I kept trying to get at the relationship between the two girls," Platt said, "But it required an enormous amount of inner dialogue. In a film, characters cannot easily say what they are feeling. But musicals allow you to 'musicalize' that inner dialogue."

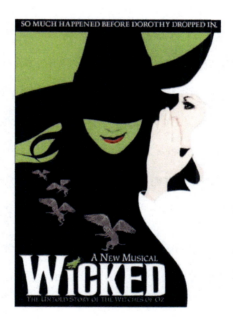

Wicked didn't immediately become a movie after Platt gained the rights for Universal. Renowned theatrical lyricist and composer Stephen Schwartz was able to gain permission from Platt to transform *Wicked* instead into a musical. Under the direction of Schwartz and Joe Mantello, the two gave a new meaning and purpose to *Wicked*.

Although the novel *Wicked* was intended to be a tragedy, the musical adaptation brimmed with witty humor and unforgettable songs. After a pre-Broadway tryout in San Francisco in May and June 2003, *Wicked* premiered at Broadway's Gershwin Theatre later that year in October.

Wicked became the surprise hit of the Broadway season, packing in audiences and becoming an all-time favorite, continuing to this day. Young people responded especially strongly to the Wicked Witch of the West/Elphaba singing "Defying Gravity" because the green girl dealt with issues they were dealing with. "It's this character that Gregory (Maguire) thought of, this green girl," said Stephen Schwartz, "We all have this green girl inside."

"If every musical had a brain, a heart, and the courage of *Wicked*, Broadway really would be a magical place," reported *TIME Magazine*.

At the 2004 Tony Awards, the original Broadway production of *Wicked* was nominated in ten categories, and Idina Menzel took home the award for Best Actress in a Musical for her portrayal of Elphaba. During her Tony acceptance speech, Idina thanked the producers for "giving the green girl a heart."

Idina Menzel with her Best Actress in a Musical Tony Award as Elphaba in the original Broadway version of *Wicked*, along with fellow winner Hugh Jackman

It took nearly three decades for Universal Pictures to bring the novel's film version of *Wicked* to life.

In 2012, Marc Platt, who initially secured the movie rights for Universal Pictures, was announced as the producer for the movie adaptation of *Wicked*. The first part of the film, which has faced delays because of COVID and the 2023 SAG-AFTRA strike, will be released in November 2024.

The movie *Wicked* was split into two parts, with a year between their releases. Director Jon M. Chu revealed how, "We decided to give ourselves a bigger canvas and make not just one *Wicked* movie but two! With more space, we can tell the story of *Wicked* as it was meant to be told while bringing even more depth and surprise to the journeys of these beloved characters."

Wicked (Part One – released Fall of 2024)

Margaret undoubtedly would have been ecstatic to see how her witch's character has evolved through the various renditions of *Wicked* and has continued to add to her incredible legacy.

Another part of Margaret's legacy occurred when Margaret's son, Hamilton (Ham) Meserve, gave a presentation about his mother at the International Wizard of Oz Club's 2009 national convention in Wamego, Kansas. Ham had never attended an Oz Club event before and was the convention's special guest of honor. While his presentation "Oz, The Witch, and Mom" was both informative and very well-received, the highlight of the convention arguably occurred at dinner.

Fellow Oz convention attendee/presenter Paul Miles Schneider (*Silver Shoes* author) was sitting at the same table as Ham and his wife Helen when Wicked Witch of the West impersonator extraordinaire Kurt Raymond entered the room in full character. Kurt went from table to table, growling and hissing at random guests in his best witch persona. Paul shared how "Ham looked at me and his wife, and he shook his head and chuckled. He then lifted the carafe of water we shared, and we started laughing amongst ourselves, knowing what he had in mind, which pretty much spurred him on to do it. So, he rose from his seat next to me while I grabbed my camera, well aware of what was coming. Kurt approached Ham with particularly targeted intent, and Ham proceeded to go after Kurt with the carafe in hand, raising it high in the air so all in the room could see him 'try' to douse Kurt with the water. Everyone roared with laughter and cheers."

Paul Miles Schneider and Ham Meserve

Ham Meserve targets The Wicked Witch of the West, aka Kurt Raymond with some water

Likewise, Ham attended another Oz-themed event at the Judy Garland Museum's 2015 festival. Once again, Ham did his presentation "Oz, The Witch, and Mom" but had no encounters with any witches at the festival.

In more recent years, Ham has continued to do presentations about his mother closer to his residence in Maine.

Perhaps no greater tribute is being paid to Margaret than the creation of the wonderful one-woman theatrical production *of My Witch: The Margaret Hamilton Stories*. The show is described as "the amazing tale of how a gentle kindergarten teacher from Cleveland became one of America's favorite character actresses and scared the living daylights out of every one of us."

Written by playwright John Ahlin for his wife and veteran actress Jean Tafler, *My Witch,* came about by accident. John told me how a review from one of his wife's plays (in which she played a female Scrooge) had compared her performance to that of Margaret Hamilton's witch character.

Intrigued by the Margaret Hamilton comparison, John and Jean decided to find out more about her career and personal life. Much to their surprise, they discovered there had never been a biography written about Margaret.[7]

Extensive research into Margaret's life revealed captivating and previously unknown information that surprised John. *My Witch,* designed as a one-woman show for Jean,

---

[7] Author's note – I cringed regarding John's comment about how NO Margaret Hamilton biography had ever been written. As I note in this book's "Prologue," I had put my book effort about her "on hold" two decades ago.

[347]

made its debut in Freeport, Maine, in October 2021. *My Witch* has been showcased in limited runs yearly since that time.

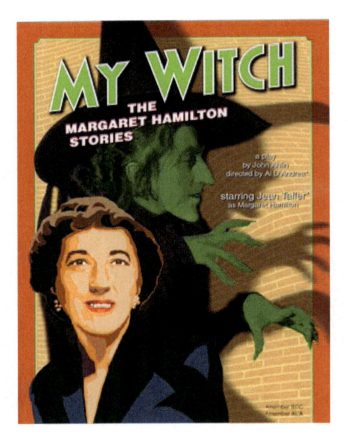

My Witch depicts Margaret Hamilton's life through several interwoven sketches. Jean assumes Margaret's persona while also impersonating some people she encountered during her memorable life. Jean's captivating performance in the show earned her many accolades.

John shared with me he hopes one day to bring *My Witch* to New York City and Cleveland – two cities with deep personal and historical ties to Margaret Hamilton - the kindest witch of all.

Jean Tafler as Margaret Hamilton in *My Witch*

I know *My Witch* will be a big hit in Cleveland. After all, for Margaret, there's no place like home.

17
MYTHS, RUMORS, AND MISCELLANEOUS

Several Margaret Hamilton items need to be debunked. Besides the incorrect belief that Margaret was the kindergarten teacher for William Windom and Jim Backus, two more recent myths have emerged.

The first item to debunk is the often-told story of how Margaret Hamilton's dachshund Otto was originally supposed to play the role of Toto. Below are two examples of actual social media posts from Instagram and Pinterest on the topic:

"The dog in The Wizard of Oz was originally supposed to be played by a Dachshund named Otto. However, the studio thought there was still too much post-war tension and replaced Otto with a Norwich terrier. This is one of the original still shots from the movie."

"Did you know a dachshund was the first dog they were planning to cast in The Wizard of Oz? The part of Toto in

The Wizard of Oz was originally meant to be played by a dachshund named Otto. **He was owned by Margaret Hamilton,** who played the part of the Wicked Witch of the West in the film. The photo of Dorothy and Otto was shot from unreleased footage of the film, where Dorothy sang 'Somewhere Over the Rainbow.'"

Otto as Toto – NOT True

Hundreds, if not thousands, of times, this false story has been shared on popular social media platforms like Facebook, Instagram, TikTok, and Pinterest. People's usual reaction to the social media post is something along the lines of "Wow - I never knew that!" and it keeps getting shared over and over again...

Research links the photoshopped picture to a prank. You can find a related post featuring Marlon Brando with the same dachshund in it.

Another item on the Internet (IMDB and Wikipedia, amongst others) lists Margaret Hamilton's first movie appearance as being in *Zoo in Budapest* in a non-credited role as an assistant orphanage matron.

NOT Margaret Hamilton's first movie role

Through watching the movie and conducting research, I found out that the role was actually played by a look-alike actress named Doro Merande. In an interview with Richard Lamparski, Margaret pointed out, "People often confused us, with our long faces and crooked noses – we actually played sisters several times." One of those times they appeared together was in the offbeat 1960s comedy *That Was the Week That Was,* in which Doro and Margaret played confused New England voters leading up to the 1964 presidential election.

Doro Merande – sometimes confused as Margaret Hamilton

Contrary to popular belief, Margaret didn't particularly like Ray Bolger all that much. Aljean Harmetz noted Margaret "felt that 'The Boys,' as she called Bolger, Lahr, and Jack Haley, had elbowed her out of their way during the making of the movie and that she never got a chance to speak when they were on the same panels. I was to keep Bolger, in particular, from answering all the questions addressed to her as well as answering his own."

Michael Patrick Hearn made similar comments about Margaret's lukewarm relationship with Bolger, and perhaps the best example of all was the letter from Margaret herself to Wesley Wehr (from his University of Washington archives) in which she writes, "I cannot STAND him!"

On a lighter note, here are a few interesting items about Margaret. She was a:

- Dues-paying member of The International Wizard of Oz Club
- Smoker until late in life
- Lifelong Republican and acquaintance of President Ronald Reagan (they were both in 1937's *Angels Wash Their Faces*)

Hough Elementary School in Cleveland (where Margaret taught kindergarten) was right down the street from

Hough Avenue Baptist Church, where Freddy Kreuger creator Wes Craven attended church as a child. Ironically, both buildings were later burned down! An interesting and fiery link between two horror film icons.

Wes Craven and Freddy Kreuger – also Cleveland icons

Hough Avenue Baptist Church – Wes Craven's
church down the street from where Margaret taught kindergarten

On one of the annual televised showings of *The Wizard of Oz* in the 1970s, Margaret Hamilton appeared in the movie as the Wicked Witch of the West and also in a Maxwell House commercial as Cora!

During the brief time Judy Garland had, from the conclusion of filming *The Wizard of Oz* to being busy out on the road promoting the movie, she visited Margaret's hometown of Cleveland while on a brief vaudeville tour.

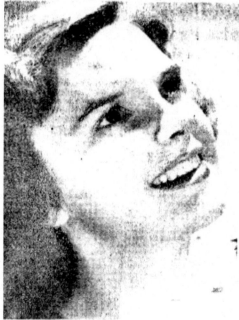

Swingsters to Visit State Friday

Loew's State is turning on its vaudeville foot-lights Friday, and its first stage star in three years will be Judy Garland, Metro's young singing prodigy. The little movie swingstress with the big voice is touring between pictures—her last one was "Listen, Darling"—and she brings a full-sized revue to brighten the State.

With her are Eddie Peabody, banjo virtuoso, and former Clevelander; the acrobatic Reiss troupe, Billy Wells and the Four Fays in tomfoolery, Stuart and Martin, all accompanied by Angelo Vitale's pit orchestra. And to start her initial visit to Cleveland off right, Judy will sing "The Star Spangled Banner" at the Indians' opening game Friday as Alva Bradley's guest when Mayor Burton pitches the first ball.

The State's picture during her engagement here next week is "Midnight," wherein the comedy is contributed by John Barrymore and a light romance by Claudette Colbert and Don Ameche. It marks the screen bow of Elaine Barrie, now known off-stage as Mrs. John Barrymore.

JUDY GARLAND

[357]

She sang "The Star-Spangled Banner" at the Cleveland Indians home baseball opener on April 21, 1939, before appearing at Cleveland's Loew's State Theater for several Vaudeville stage shows. There is no truth to the rumor that Margaret flew by on her broom after the singing of the National Anthem.

Judy Sings National Anthem

Judy Garland, sixteen-year-old movie star, sings "The Star Spangled Banner" in the flag-raising ceremony at the Indians' opener in the stadium yesterday. She closes her ears to echoes.

ACKNOWLEDGEMENTS

I'd like to express my gratitude to the many individuals who have supported me throughout my book journey. They can be classified into two separate categories, with a twenty-year gap between them. A posthumous thank you is owed to Michael Heaton from *The Plain Dealer* for his initial contributions (as explained in the Prologue), which laid the foundation for the inception of this book.

Growing up in Cleveland, just like Margaret, gave me a unique advantage in delving into her early life through research. My heartfelt thanks go out to the many fellow Clevelanders and their organizations, who played a pivotal role in granting me access to the information presented in this book. From this initial group of people 20 years ago, I would like to thank these folks:

Pam Fife	Hathaway Brown High School
Nan Matern	The Cleveland Play House
Jennifer Steirer	The Cleveland Junior League
Kristy Sharpe	Wheelock College
Holly Timm	Genealogy Society

The assistance provided by the staff at the Cleveland Public Library, spanning two decades, has been nothing short of amazing. Librarians rock! The librarians at the New York Public Library, University of Washington, Columbus, and Greenwich libraries also receive this recognition.

More recently, I'd like to thank the following folks from Cleveland:

Maggie Milano	The Cleveland Play House
Eleanor Blackman	Kelvin Smith Library
Rick Horvath	Bratenahl Historical Society

Esteemed local author Rick Porrello, known for his book *To Kill the Irishman*, graciously offered valuable feedback on various subjects.

Thank you to Michele at the Everett Collection, the staff at Alamy, and The Andy Warhol Museum for their help and patience in licensing the many photos used in the book.

My editors, including my son Ken, Frank Wallace, and John D., deserve a special mention for their exceptional contributions. They not only helped me rectify my grammar and spelling errors, but also offered valuable suggestions and unique insights.

Special thanks to artist extraordinaire Julia Ruprecht for stepping in at the last minute to provide some wonderful sketches.

Noted Oz authors Michael Patrick Hearn and Paul Miles Schneider provided marvelous stories and material used in my book. In addition to providing great feedback, Oz historian and author Bill Stillman even took the time to review part of my manuscript, specifically the section about Margaret and her performance in *The Wizard of Oz*.

Special thanks to the following individuals who generously shared their captivating stories of meeting Margaret and, in some instances, provided valuable items featured in the book: Carl Anthony, Randy Ward, Ken Rowe, Beth (from Sardi's), and Mark Ryan.

Likewise, I received valuable input from Jane Albright and Peter Hanff of The International Wizard of Oz Club, as well as John Kelsch and Brian Carlson from the Judy Garland Museum.

I received much-appreciated and interesting feedback from Jenna, who put together the outstanding William Windom Tribute site, along with Angela from The Friends of Linden Hill.

Adam, from the Academy of Motion Picture Arts and Sciences Film Archive, generously dedicated his time and expertise to assist me with my research request.

Finally, special thanks to John Ahlin, Katherine Quinn, and Astrid King, who provided rare information related to Margaret.

SOURCES

BOOKS

Baum, Frank L., *The Wizard of Oz*, Lewes, England: Unicorn Publishing House, 1985

Baum, Frank L., *The Wonderful Wizard of Oz*, Chicago: George M. Hill, 1900

Bawden, James and Miller, Ron. *Conversations with Classic Film Stars*. Lexington, KY: University Press of Kentucky, 2016.

Bellamy, Ralph. *When The Smoke Hit the Fan*. Garden City, NY: Doubleday and Company, 1979.

Brideson, Cynthia. Also Starring...: *Forty Biographical Essays on the Greatest Character Actors of Hollywood's Golden Era, 1930-1965*. Orlando, FL: BearManor Media, 2012.

Brodek, Lorraine. *A Nobody in a Somebody World*. Mustang, OK: Tate Publishing, 2013.

Burke, Billie. *With a Feather on My Nose*. New York: Appleton-Century-Crofts, 1949.

Danforth, Roger. *The Cleveland Play House: 1915-1990.* Divernon, IL: Emerson Press, 1990.

Flory, Julia. *The Cleveland Play House: 1915-1927.* Cleveland: Press of the Western Reserve, 1965.

Frank, Gerold. *Judy.* New York: Harper & Row, 1975.

Franken, Rose. *When All I Said and Done.* Garden City, NY: Doubleday and Company, 1963.

Fricke, John, Scarfone, Jay, Stillman, William. *The Wizard of Oz: The Official 50th Anniversary Pictorial History.* New York: Warner Books, 1989.

Fricke, John. *Judy Garland: A Portrait in Art and Anecdote.* New York: Bullfinch Press, 2003.

Griffin, Merv. *Merv: An Autobiography.* New York: Pocket Books, 1981.

Harmetz, Aljean. *The Making of The Wizard of Oz.* New York: Hyperion, 1998.

Hayter-Menzies, Grant. Mrs. Ziegfeld: The Public and Private Lives of Billie Burke. *Jefferson, N.C.: McFarland & Company, 2009.*

Heitmann, Robert. *Best Witches.* Racine, WI: Golden Press, 1960.

Herbert, Ian. *Who's Who in the Theatre.* Detroit: Pitman, 1977.

Herbst, Dorothy. *A History of the Cleveland Play House from its origin to September 1936*. Chicago: Northwestern University, 1937.

Juran, Robert. *Old Familiar Faces*. Sarasota, Fl: Movie Memories Publishing, 1995.

Keeshan, Bob. *Growing Up Happy*. Garden City, NY: Doubleday and Company, 1989.

Luft, Lorna. *Me and My Shadows: A Family Memoir*. New York: Simon and Schuster, 1998.

Marx, Bill. *Son of Harpo Speaks!* Orlando, FL: BearManor Media, 2010.

McClelland, Doug. *Down the Yellow Brick Road: The Making of The Wizard of Oz*. New York: Putnam Publishing Group, 1976.

McGill, Raymond. *Notable Names in the American Theater*. Clifton, NJ: JT White, 1976.

Moritz, Charles. *Current Biography Yearbook 1979*. New York: H.W. Wilson Company, 1980.

Nissen, Axel. *Accustomed to Her Face: Thirty-Five Character Actresses of Golden Age Hollywood*. Jefferson, NC: McFarland & Co., 2016.

Oldenburg, Chloe Warner. *Leaps of Faith: History of The Cleveland Play House: 1915-85*. Cleveland: 1985.

Scarfone, Jay, Stillman, William. *The Road to Oz*. Essex, CT: Lyons Press, 2018.

Scarfone, Jay, Stillman, William. *The Wizard of Oz: The Official 75th Anniversary Companion*. New York: Harper, 2013.

Scarfone, Jay, Stillman, William. *The Wizardry of Oz: The Artistry and Magic of the 1939 MGM Classic*. New York: Applause Books, 2004.

Shatner, William. *Up Till Now: The Autobiography*. New York: St. Martin's Griffin, 2009.

Tibbetts, John. *American Classic Screen Interviews*. Lanham, MD: Scarecrow Press, 2010.

Twomey, Alfred and McClure, Arthur. *The Versatiles*. New York: A.S. Barnes, 1969.

Van Leuven, Holly. *Ray Bolger: More Than a Scarecrow*. New York: Oxford University Press, 2019

Vermilye, Jerry. *Movie Buffs Book*. New York: Pyramid, 1975.

Warhol Andy. *The Andy Warhol Diaries*. New York: Warner Books, 1989.

Wehr, Wesley. *The Eighth Lively Art*. Seattle: University of Washington Press, 2000.

Willingham, Elaine. *Cooking in Oz*, Nashville: Cumberland Press, 1999.

Windom, William. *Journeyman Actor*. Bloomington, In.: iUniverse, 2009.

NEWSPAPERS AND MAGAZINES

Admission Magazine of Hathaway Brown School
Atlanta Constitution
Berkshire Eagle
Beverly Hills Weekly Magazine
Bridgeport Post
Bristol Courier
Brooklyn Daily Eagle
Cleveland Bystander
Cleveland News
Cleveland Press
Cleveland Town Topics
Connecticut Western News
Hollywood Magazine
Hollywood Reporter
Kennebunk Post
Kenosha News
L.A. Times

Lewiston Sun Maine Journal

Millbrook Round Table

Newsday

New York Herald Tribune

New York Post

New York Times

New York World-Telegram

Oakland Tribune

Parade Magazine

People Magazine

The Plain Dealer

Playthings

Rochester Post Bulletin

Screenland

Standard Star

St. Louis Post

Time Magazine

Variety

Westchester Rockland Newspaper

White Plains Reporter Dispatch

Wilmington Journal

Yankee Magazine

INTERNET RESOURCES

1894 Cuyahoga County Biographies

American Film Institute

Bratenahl Historical Society / Notable People

Cinekyd Margaret Hamilton Interview

Fred Barton Website

Internet Broadway Database

Internet Movie Database

Judy Garland Museum

Judy Garland News

The Judy Room

Richard Lamparksi: Whatever Became of Margaret Hamilton? (radio interview)

Mego Corporation

Sons of the Desert

Summit Metro Parks

Western Reserve Historical Society

William Windom Tribute Site

CDS AND MOVIES

The Wizard of Oz (Three-Disc Collector's Edition) 2004

An Evening with the Wicked Witch of the West

Brian Carlson with The Judy Garland Museum 1979 CD

INTERVIEWS/CORRESPONDENCE

John Ahlin

Jane Albright

Carl Anthony

Brian Carlson

Peter Hanff

Michael Patrick Hearn

John Kelsch

Astrid King

Katherine Quinn

Ken Rowe

Mark Ryan

Paul Miles Schneider

Bill Stillman

Randy Ward

MISCELLANEOUS

Academy of Motion Picture Arts and Sciences Film Archive

Bedside Network

Cape Playhouse Archives

Cleveland Play House Archives

Cleveland Public Library

Collection of Cleveland Play House programs

Theatre Collection biographies

Microfilm archives

Columbus Public Library

Friends of Linden Hill

Greenwich Library

Hathaway Brown High School 1921 Yearbook

Lakewood Theatre Archives

New York Public Library Archive, Margaret Hamilton Correspondence and Ephemera

Newberry Library Archives

Sardi's in Manhattan

Spotlight Newsletter, Summer, 2010. Series 7, Box: 92, Folder: 4. Cleveland Play House Archive, Kelvin Smith Library Special Collections, Case Western Reserve University

University of Washington, Wesley Wehr Archives

Wheelock College Archives

PHOTO CREDITS

Cover: courtesy of the Everett Collection. All Rights Reserved; p. 10: IanDagnall Computing / Alamy Stock Photo; p. 18: AA Film Archive / Alamy Stock Photo; p. 36: Keystone Pictures USA / Alamy Stock Photos; p. 38: copyright Hathaway Brown; used by permission; p.43: copyright Wheelock College; used by permission; p. 52: Album / Alamy Stock Photo; p. 55: Album / Alamy Stock Photo; chapters 3 and 14: Cleveland Playhouse Archives; used by permission. All rights reserved.; p. 67: Chronicle / Alamy Stock Photo; p. 85 – 87: copyright Cape Playhouse; used by permission; p. 105: Cinematic Collection / Alamy Stock Photo; p. 109: FOX Pictures / RGR Collection / Alamy Stock Photo; p. 109: Sportsphoto Entertainers / Alamy Stock Photo; p. 111: Everett Collection / Alamy Stock Photo; p. 112: Courtesy: Everett Collection. All Rights Reserved; p. 122: Courtesy: Everett Collection. All Rights Reserved; p. 125: Courtesy: Everett Collection. All Rights Reserved; p. 127: AA Film Archive / Alamy Stock Photos; p. 130: AA Film Archive / Alamy Stock Photo; p. 133: Pictorial Press / Alamy Stock Photo; p. 141:

Photo 12 / Alamy Stock Photo; p. 145: Moviestore Collection / Alamy Stock Photo; p. 146 Collection Christopher / Alamy Stock Photo; p. 150: Courtesy: Everett Collection. All Rights Reserved; p. 151: Courtesy: Everett Collection. All Rights Reserved; p. 152: Courtesy: Everett Collection. All Rights Reserved; p. 153: Courtesy: Everett Collection. All Rights Reserved; p.158: Archive PL / Alamy Stock Photo; p. 159: Courtesy: Everett Collection. All Rights Reserved; p. 164: Rajko Sumunovic / Alamy Stock Photo; p. 165 – 167: Andy Warhol *The Witch*, 1981 from the *Myths* portfolio screenprint with diamond dust on Lenox Museum board 38 x 38 inches. Courtesy Ronald Feldman Gallery, New York. © The Andy Warhol Foundation for the Visual Arts / Artists Rights Society (ARS), New York / Ronald Feldman Gallery, New York; p. 170: TCD/Prod DB / Alamy Stock Photo; p. 176: Album / Alamy Stock Photo; p. 185: Everett Collection. All Rights Reserved; p. 187: Everett Collection. All Rights Reserved; p. 189: Archive PL / Alamy Stock Photo; p. 191: AA Film Archive / Alamy Stock Photo; p. 192: Impress / Alamy Stock Photo; p. 193: Shirlaine Forrest via Getty Images; p. 196: Screenland Magazine; p. 199: All Star Picture Library / Alamy Stock Photo; p. 201: Album / Alamy Stock

Photo; p. 202: Everett Collection. All Rights Reserved; p. 205: Universal Pictures / RGR Collection / Alamy Stock Photo; p. 205: WFPA / Alamy Stock Photo; p. 208 – 210: copyright Lakewood Theatre Archives / Katherine Quinn; used by permission; p. 216: Album / Alamy Stock Photo; p. 219, 286, 345, and 346 copyright Paul Miles Schneider; used by permission; p. 220: Maximum Film / Alamy Stock Photo; p. 232: copyright Newberry Library Archive; used by permission; p. 233: Archive PL / Alamy Stock Photo; p. 214, 237 - 241 copyright Astrid King; used by permission; p. 244: All Rights Reserved. Courtesy: NYPL Billy Rose Archive Collection; p. 246: Cinematic Collection / Alamy Stock Photo; p. 249: Everett Collection. All Rights Reserved; p. 251 and 258: All Rights Reserved. Courtesy: NYPL Billy Rose Archive Collection; p. 261: Phillip Harrington / Alamy Stock Photo; p. 263: Everett Collection. All Rights Reserved; p. 270: copyright Carl Anthony; used by permission; p. 272, 320, and 321 copyright Peter Hanff; used by permission; p. 273: copyright Linden Hill Estate; used by permission; p. 280 and 281 copyright Michael Patrick Hearn; used by permission; p. 289: copyright Ken Rowe; used by permission; p. 290: All Rights Reserved. Courtesy: Judy Garland Museum; p.

300: The Picture Art Collection / Alamy Stock Photo; p. 301: Zuma / Alamy Stock Photo; p. 301: Pictorial Press / Alamy Stock Photo; p. 304: copyright Cleveland Play House Archive, Kelvin Smith Library Special Collections, Case Western Reserve University; used by permission; p. 305: Everett Collection. All Rights Reserved; p. 311: Cinematic Collection / Alamy Stock Photo; p. 312: Album / Alamy Stock Photo; p. 313: TCD/Prod DB / Alamy Stock Photo; p. 314: Columbia Pictures / RGR Collection / Alamy Stock Photo; p. 315: Archive PL / Alamy Stock Photo; p. 316: TCD/Prod DB / Alamy Stock Photo; p. 317: Archive PL / Alamy Stock Photo; p. 319: copyright John Kelsch: used by permission; p. 322: copyright Jane Albright; used by permission; p. 325 and 326: copyright Mark Ryan; used by permission; p. 327: copyright Sardi's; used by permission; p. 329: All Rights Reserved. Courtesy: NYPL Billy Rose Archive Collection; p. 339: Patti McConville / Alamy Stock Photo; p. 341: Ezio Petersen / Alamy Stock Photo; p. 343: BFA / Alamy Stock Photo; p. 348 and 349: copyright John Ahlin; used by permission; p. 353: SilverScreen / Alamy Stock Photo; p. 354: Collection Christopher / Alamy Stock Photo; p. 356: Featureflash

Archive / Alamy Stock Photo and Pictorial Press / Alamy Stock Photo.

A BRIEF NOTE

Little did author **DON BILLIE** realize when he was writing for the aptly named *Cleveland State Cauldron* that one day, he'd be uncovering the enchanting tale of Margaret Hamilton, Cleveland's very own Wicked Witch of the West.

Mr. Billie, who has previously written about the Cleveland origin of Freddy Kreuger for *Cleveland Magazine*, is also the author of *Hey You Punks!*, a book that vividly depicts his experiences growing up on Cleveland's gritty near west side.

To embody the principles of *The Wizard of Oz* as a "good deed doer," he has dedicated his time to volunteering with both The American Red Cross hurricane disaster relief effort in Florida and the humanitarian organization Bring Hope in refugee camps affected by war in Iraqi Kurdistan.

Cleveland Browns Superfan "Big Willie," the author, and a rabid member of the Dawg Pound, bring some real "CLE" cred to the table

Illustrator Julia Ruprecht is a passionate artist who has a flair for storytelling through the use of color and creativity. She has an extensive background in illustration and has collaborated with many talented authors on projects ranging from children's books to young adult novels. A native of Cleveland, Ohio, Julia lives with her greatest muse and inspiration: her cat Pepper and is constantly working on her next project.

Printed in Great Britain
by Amazon